SHORT SERMONS
FOR PREACHERS
ON THE RUN

Short Sermons for Preachers on the Run

WALTER J. BURGHARDT

ORBIS BOOKS
Maryknoll, New York 10545

Copyright © 2009 by Orbis Books.

Published by Orbis Books, Maryknoll, NY 10545-0308.

Manufactured in the United States of America.

Library of Congress Cataloging-in-Publication Data

Burghardt, Walter J.
    Short sermons for preachers on the run / Walter J. Burghardt.
      p. cm.
    ISBN 978-1-57075-848-5 (pbk.)
    1. Catholic Church – Sermons. 2. Sermons, American – 21st century. 3. Occasional sermons – Catholic Church. I. Title.
  BX1756.B828S55 2009
  252′.02 – dc22

                                    2009007234

Contents

Part Three
SPECIAL FEASTS AND MEMORIALS

Part Four
CELEBRATIONS

Part Five
TRIBUTE

Foreword

When I was stepping down as pastor of Holy Trinity parish in Washington, D.C., a parishioner, Natalie Ganley, wife and mother, gifted writer and skilled retreat director, said to me, "I'll really miss your homilies — not the Sunday homilies, but your weekday homilies." I didn't know whether to feel delighted or deflated. I spent hours preparing my Sunday homilies, and like Walter Burghardt, my homiletic hero, I wrote out every word and throughout the previous week returned to the text incessantly to polish, polish, polish. My weekday homilies, on the other hand, were a grab bag of insights and inspirations gleaned from my morning meditations on the Scripture texts of the day. I never wrote out those homilies. Bullets on a half-sheet had to do. The style was conversational, and the time limit was five minutes max.

As soon as I started to read this present collection of homilies, I said to myself, "These are Walter's 'weekday' homilies, even those preached on Sunday." And what Natalie said to me I said to Walter, as he gazed down from heaven, "Walter, we are really going to miss your homilies — I mean your 'weekday' homilies!"

Why? It is because these brief, informal, and conversational homilies open wide a window into Walter's faith, hope, and caring — into Walter himself — in a way his Sunday homilies rarely, if ever, do. The "him" we see in his "weekday homilies" is wise but occasionally opinionated. His hopeful outlook on life soars high, though a struggling doubt peeks through at times. He calls us to direct hands-on service to the poor but admits that he himself remains the contemplative scholar and writer. His quick wit and quirky turn of phrase accompany a passionate seriousness about arousing us to the self-sacrificing love of Christ, to which Walter himself was totally surrendered. In a word, we meet here the very human Walter Burghardt in all his grandeur and all his simplicity. Brilliant as they are, his "Sunday" homilies never opened that window nearly so wide.

It was in his nineties that Walter preached these brief, insightful homilies. He was almost blind from macular degeneration. He had grown slow of foot, but never of mind. In these homilies we recognize a voice lively to the end, thanks, I am sure, to the fact that his heart remained ever alive with the love of God and concern for all the rest of us.

At Walter's request, I preached the homily at his funeral Mass. It is the last homily in this collection. It shares reflections on Walter the scholar, Walter the man, and Walter the passionate preacher of social justice. For Walter I prepared a "Sunday" homily — even including three carefully delineated points!

"Tolle et lege!" an angel of light said to St. Augustine, thereby launching his conversion. "Take and read!" I say to you about this collection of homilies. I am sure you will find them most rewarding — maybe even converting!

James L. Connor, S.J.
Provincial Assistant for Mission and Renewal
Maryland Province of the Society of Jesus
Baltimore, Maryland

Short Sermons for Preachers on the Run

Introduction

This book of homilies needs an introduction because it differs significantly in content from the fourteen volumes that preceded it. Earlier homilies probed deeply and at some length, usually five or six printed pages. Scriptural scholars and theological experts were summoned for support, with pertinent documentation in endnotes. Such material, a source of continuing education for many a pulpit devotee, is harshly limited in the present volume for the ease of the preacher on the run.

Each homily in the older volumes had been fully developed and had been preached by me on a liturgical occasion, e.g., a wedding or Sunday Mass. Not so the present collection. The first homily represents my former style: longer in length and more specific examples in each of my notorious three points of earlier years.

As a young Jesuit I found myself at home and with expertise in patristics, the area of theology focusing on the early church fathers. Recently I reminisced on the warmth of those days through a portion of Ben-Zion Gold's *The Life of Jews in Poland before the Holocaust*. Rabbi Gold's reflections on his childhood reminded me of my own searching and satisfaction among the church fathers:

> The weekly Torah reading brought us closer to the persons who appeared in it. We felt as if the patriarchs

were our great-grandparents. We shared their joys and sorrows. Each year we experienced anew the drama of Joseph and his brothers. I felt ashamed that the fathers of the Jewish tribes were cruel toward their brother and mindless about causing grief to their father. Two weeks later when we read the sidra "Vayigash," with the story of their reconciliation, I was thrilled by Joseph's generosity toward his brothers. The "family" was whole again. . . .

Two thousand years of weekly Torah reading had inspired the development of an extensive library of commentaries. . . . All the commentaries brought to the sidra [weekly Torah reading] the beliefs and dilemmas of their time, and together they reflect Jewish thought through the ages.

The Humash (the five books of Moses) that we used had the commentaries of Rashi from eleventh-century France; of Ibn Ezra from twelfth-century Spain; of Nahmanides, a near contemporary of Ibn Ezra from Barcelona; of Rashbam, a grandson of Rashi; and of Sforno from fifteenth-century Italy. These commentators, who lived at different times and places, referred to each other as if they were contemporaries at a round table.[1]

For decades I prepared my homilies as though they were in some sense collaborative efforts of all the theologians I had studied who came before me as well as contemporaries who continued to labor with me. I would grab from my bookshelves the tome of an ancient writer while, at the same time, insights of other theologians were striking new chords in my heart and mind. Scripture scholars, especially Sulpician Raymond E. Brown and fellow Jesuit Joseph A. Fitzmyer, were never far from my desk. Vying for my attention, poets kept poking their way to the top of my reading pile, and classical composers broke the silence of my room.

In thinking about this set of homilies, I was forced to acknowledge a pressing reality. Over the past half century, Catholic pastors — often with no assistant — have been called on to minister to increasing spiritual and material needs of parishioners. Lock your mind onto some of the data compiled by CARA (Center for Applied Research in the Apostolate), located at Georgetown University, Washington, D.C.[2]

U.S. DATA	1965	1985	2005
Total priests	**58,632**	**57,317**	**42,839**
Diocesan priests	35,925	35,052	28,702
Religious priests	22,707	22,265	14,137
Priestly ordinations	**994**	**533**	**454**
Permanent deacons	**n/a**	**7,204**	**14,574**
Parishes	**17,637**	**19,244**	**18,891**
Without resident priest	549	1,051	3,251

It is not solely seeing the last column above with its startling statistics that moved me to change substantially my method of writing homilies. Equally startling is the impact on clergy and laity stemming from the decrease in number of priests and consequent increase in number of parishes without a resident priest. One example: a growing number of homilists do not have the amount of time I have had over my many years to weigh and weave words.

Homilists one and all: begin by contrasting sermons 1 and 2. The first never before published I delivered in 1993 at a wedding of one of my cousins. The second was written fourteen years later and exemplifies the differences in length and style of homilies and "sermonettes" many priests have been forced to deliver because of increased demands on their time and energy.

Over the years I was told that from time to time various preachers used my texts usually without reference to me. Now I say to all of you, "Shed the guilt!" This volume is a gift to busy clergy, to preachers on the run. Take these homilies and use them as they are here or change them to fit better the lives of your own parishioners. Sadly, time constraints may keep you from getting to know intimately the early church fathers. Nonetheless, you are not alone. My words and wishes are with you but hopefully not as forcefully as the Word of God continues to be in your own lives.

Walter J. Burghardt, S.J.
Manresa Hall
Merion Station, Pennsylvania
Maryland Province of the Society of Jesus
September 17, 2007

Note: In November 2005, I moved to Merion Station, Pennsylvania (literally across the street from Philadelphia) into Manresa Hall, a residence for Jesuits in need of short- or long-term medical assistance. Because much of this book was written here, in this text most references to Manresa pertain to this particular place. Mention of the "other" Manresa — where the founder of the Society of Jesus, St. Ignatius of Loyola, spent several months in prayer — is designated by including its location, Spain.

PART ONE

WEDDINGS

1

If I Have Not Love...

A Wedding Homily

Then the Lord God said, "It is not good that the man should be alone; I will make him a helper as his partner." So out of the ground the Lord God formed every animal of the field and every bird of the air, and brought them to the man to see what he would call them; and whatever the man called each living creature, that was its name. The man gave names to all cattle, and to the birds of the air, and to every animal of the field; but for the man there was not found a helper as his partner. So the Lord God caused a deep sleep to fall upon the man, and he slept; then he took one of his ribs and closed up its place with flesh. And the rib that the Lord God had taken from the man he made into a woman and brought her to the man. Then the man said,

> *"This at last is bone of my bones*
>   *and flesh of my flesh;*
> *this one shall be called Woman,*
>   *for out of Man this one was taken."*

Therefore a man leaves his father and his mother and clings to his wife, and they become one flesh. —Gen. 2:18–24

But strive for the greater gifts. And I will show you a still more excellent way.

If I speak in the tongues of mortals and of angels, but do not have love, I am a noisy gong or a clanging cymbal. And if I have prophetic powers, and understand all mysteries and all knowledge, and if I have all faith, so as to remove mountains, but do not have love, I am nothing. If I give away all my possessions, and if I hand over my body so that I may boast, but do not have love, I gain nothing.

Love is patient; love is kind; love is not envious or boastful or arrogant or rude. It does not insist on its own way; it is not irritable or resentful; it does not rejoice in wrongdoing, but rejoices in the truth. It bears all things, believes all things, hopes all things, endures all things.

Love never ends. But as for prophecies, they will come to an end; as for tongues, they will cease; as for knowledge, it will come to an end.   —1 Cor. 12:31—13:8

"This is my commandment, that you love one another as I have loved you. No one has greater love than this, to lay down one's life for one's friends. You are my friends if you do what I command you. I do not call you servants any longer, because the servant does not know what the master is doing; but I have called you friends, because I have made known to you everything that I have heard from my Father. You did not choose me but I chose you."   —John 15:12–16a

Michelle and Chris: On a wedding day two problems plague a preacher. On the one hand, everything worth saying has seemingly been said — perhaps best by poets. On the other hand, no one but you two can actually say what should be said — if only because you say it not with naked syllables but with your eyes, your touch, your life.

Still, you have eased my "mission impossible." The readings you have chosen from God's own Book suggest, share with us, what this day means to you. All three texts focus on oneness, on love, but in different ways. Genesis tells us how love began; Paul tells us how love grows; Jesus tells us how love peaks. A word on each.

I

Genesis tells us how love began. Not God's love, but ours. Here listen carefully, for you may have missed the mystery. After fashioning the first man, the Lord declares, "It is not good that the man should be alone; I will make him a helper as his partner," someone corresponding to him, a counterpart (Gen. 2:18). What does God do? God brings to Adam the beasts and birds just now created. Why? To have Adam "name" them. In the Hebrew mentality, for Adam to "name" something was for Adam to recognize its nature, see it for what it is, give it the meaning it had for Adam in this world. And what does the first man see? Not one of these creatures of field or sky — however graceful and gentle, however lovely and lovable — is fit for him, suitable for him, can complement him, complete his being. Yes, they are like him: They see and hear, touch and taste and smell. But they are not like enough to him. Is the Lord frustrated? Not at all. God shapes a creature at once different from the man and strikingly similar. So similar that Scripture in a burst of high imagination pictures God fashioning the other out of the man's very body. But don't be distracted by poetic detail: Adam is not really losing a rib; he is gaining a woman.

Now note Adam's reaction. When the first man sets eyes on the first woman, he exclaims in ecstasy, "This at last is bone of my bones and flesh of my flesh . . . !" (v. 23). "This one" — three times he shouts it — here is man's joyous surprise as he welcomes his one equal on earth, his peer and companion. Here, the author adds, is an affinity, an attraction, so strong that it will loosen the strongest bonds in early life, the bonds that bind to parents and home. "Therefore a man leaves his father and his mother and clings to his wife, and they become one flesh" (v. 24).

So in Scripture's symbolic description did love begin, the love of man and woman. It began with God. A God of high imagination. So imaginative that God invented not one image of God but two — similar in shape and spirit, yet not the same. What does this demand of you? That while remaining two, you increasingly become one. At times submerging but never surrendering what makes you your own person, your precious self, you enrich that self with the other, enrich the other with your self. From your first kiss as husband and wife, through your different careers, to your supreme act of love, whatever you do is a "yes" to the other. Very simply, there is indeed "I and thou," but never "mine and thine."

II

If Genesis tells us how love began, Paul tells us how love grows. Paul has a "thing" about love, is almost obsessed by it; without love your life and mine have no meaning whatsoever. Listen to him. If I can speak (or even preach) like an angel — the way, say, the angel Gabriel announced to Mary that she was selected to mother God's Son — but there is no love in me, I'm a windbag, a New Year's noise-maker. If I own the world's clearest crystal ball, can predict everything from the first snowfall to the Eagles in the Super Bowl; if my faith is powerful enough to move the Allegheny Mountains from Pennsylvania to Sparta, New Jersey;[3] if my intellect can grasp God Three-in-One and the billions of stars in outer space — with all this, if I "do not have love, I am nothing" (1 Cor. 13:2). And suppose, in the spirit of Francis of Assisi, I give every last item I own to Mother Teresa for her Indian outcasts, let Christian haters burn me at the stake — "if I do not have love, I gain nothing" (v. 3), not one jot, not one iota. In God's eyes, no love, no Chris, no Michelle . . . just nothing.

Strong language indeed, frightening. But that paragraph in Paul is only one side of the coin. The other side, Paul's next paragraph, is the scene you and I are privileged to share this afternoon. With God's help, Michelle and Chris promise, they will be "patient . . . kind" (v. 4), even when nerves fray from socks in the bathroom to different appreciations of the Navy. They will not be "envious or boastful or arrogant or rude" (vv. 4–5), because each is so sensitive to the image of God in the other, is aware that we all image an infinite God in infinitely different ways, knows that difference need not divide, can blend into a superb symphony if only love conducts. They will refuse to "insist on [their] own way" (v. 5) — possible though the peril is, especially as the years stiffen not only their muscles but their minds — if only they do not forget that two-in-one demands indeed "I and thou" but forbids "mine and thine."

A word of warning here. This kind of love, the love that "bears all things, believes all things, hopes all things, endures all things" (v. 7), is not a love Michelle and Chris can manufacture in their own private lab, by their high IQs, buoyant personalities, keen sensitivity, even delightful if weird senses of humor. The love Paul praises, the love he sings so lyrically, leaps light-years beyond those wondrous traits. It is the love Paul proclaimed to the Christians of Rome: ". . . hope does not disappoint us, because God's love has been poured into our hearts through the Holy Spirit who has been given to us" (Rom. 5:5). What offers precious promise for Paul's kind of love, for a love that will never end, is God's love. Not somewhere in outer space but deep inside of you. The God who shaped you in His likeness, the God who brought you together against all the odds, this same God lives within you. And, wonder of wonders, this loving Father's only Son, who bloodied a cross to link you like this in love, will soon nestle in your palms, cradle on your tongues, home in your hearts. Such is the love that pervades you today; such is the love I pray will only grow through the years that beckon ahead.

III

Now if Genesis tells us how love began, and Paul tells us how love grows, Jesus tells how love peaks. Granted that God made you, Chris and Michelle, for each other, granted that your love has come down to us from a rich Christian tradition — a tradition confirmed by the best of modern psychology: "A love that is not for more than itself will die.... Over the long haul an intimate relationship ... which doesn't reach outward will stagnate."[4]

You see, turning together to others should have two splendid effects. First, it might well make the difference between a marriage that is ceaselessly exciting and a marriage that the years turn into a rut, a routine, dull as dishwater, "b o r i n g." You need others. Not as a distraction, a diversion, an escape from your housemate, marriage as an endless cocktail party. Rather, to strengthen your love, to fill it out, to people it with men and women who are part and parcel of your love. I mean men and women such as surround you at this moment, who have played some part (bit parts and feature roles) in your coming together, without whom the years that lie ahead could be lonely indeed, a terrible risk. And I mean untold men and women you have not yet met, who will touch your lives in ways not yet known.

Second effect: If you turn your love to others, you will change the acre of God's world on which you dance so lightly. You deliberately chose as your wedding Gospel the solemn command of Jesus, "Love one another [love others] as I have loved you" (John 15:12). The other you are ordered to love has many faces — contrasting faces: ruddy with health or wasted with hunger, hearty with hope or bowed in despair, comfortable in condos or shivering in shelters, basking on beaches or bound behind bars, living lavishly or existing below the poverty line, greeting each day with song in the shower or dreading each inhuman dawn. All of these you are commanded to love — not invited, commanded; and to love each and all as Jesus loves you. And how has Jesus loved you? Unto crucifixion. Recall your Gospel: "No one has greater love than this, to lay down one's life" for another (John 15:13).

Such love is a "mission impossible" if you try it alone: a Rambo and a Wonder Woman conquering "hell and high water" by muscle and wit, by superbrains and technology. No. Your presence here, your vows in so sacred a spot, your communion in the blood of Christ — this whispers to the world that your hope for happiness rests not so much in what you have made of yourselves, rests far more in a God who wore your flesh to experience your pain, who died that you might live life to the full.

Yes, God will be with you. But not only God. This congregation gathers here because in varied ways our love has touched you, has helped bring you to this moment. But there is more. Our presence is a promise. A promise that, however many the miles that part us, we shall never be far from you. Even when our eyes meet not, you will be alive in us: in our hearts ever warm to you, in our hands ever outstretched to you, in our prayers that wing to heaven for you.

A final word, good friends all. What Michelle and Chris need in a special way is the example of men and women who for one year or fifty have grown in wedded love, through thick and thin, through pleasure and pain, through agony and ecstasy. And so, a few moments from now, when Chris and Michelle join hands and hearts forever, I would ask the wedded among you to link your own hands and softly murmur to each other, to the world around you, to the God within you the words that years have enriched with experience: "I take you for better for worse, for richer for poorer, in sickness and in health, till death do us part. I will love you and honor you as long as we both shall live."

No greater gift can all of us give this couple we love so dearly: for in this gift we will be promising them...our very selves.

2

Love: Only for Two?

A Wedding Charge

This is my commandment, that you love one another as I have loved you. No one has greater love than this, to lay down one's life for one's friends. —John 15:12–13

Then the righteous will answer him and say, "Lord, when was it that we saw you hungry and gave you food, or thirsty and gave you something to drink? And when was it that we saw you a stranger and welcomed you, or naked and gave you clothing? And when was it that we saw you sick or in prison, and visited you?" And the king will answer them, "Truly, I tell you, just as you did it to one of these who are members of my family, you did it for me." —Matt. 25:37–40

I commend to you two commands that stem not from this aging Jesuit but from an ageless Jesus. But not to worry! For, as King Henry VIII said to each of his wives, "I shall not keep you very long."

I

The first command all but leaped from the lips of Jesus: "This is my commandment, that you love one another as

I have loved you" (John 15:12). The words were indeed spoken to Jesus' immediate disciples, but they surely apply to disciples like Andrew and Blakey. And how will you two love each other as Jesus loves you? If your love for each other is a total gift, all you have, all you are, all you hope to be. But this is only half the picture.

II

A second command stems in part from a natural conviction that a love that is imprisoned in the lovers and does not expand to a tortured world is in danger of self-destruction. This thesis fits well with Jesus' description of those who at the Last Judgment will inherit his kingdom:

> "For I was hungry and you gave me food, I was thirsty and you gave me something to drink, I was a stranger and you welcomed me, I was naked and you gave me clothing, I was sick and you took care of me, I was in prison and you visited me." Then the righteous will answer him and say, "Lord, when was it that we saw you hungry and gave you food, or thirsty and gave you something to drink? And when was it that we saw you a stranger and welcomed you, or naked and gave you clothing? And when was it that we saw you sick or in prison, and visited you?" And the king will answer them, "Truly, I tell you, just as you did it to one of these who are members of my family, you did it for me." (Matt. 25:35–40)

III

Good friends: this day we are graced to experience a striking example of response to Jesus' twin commands to love. For in both Blakey and Andrew we can now recognize not only a profoundly personal love. We discover also their love reaching out to untold others.

Time and space forbid biographies. What sufficed for me, what impressed me, was learning that each is a director in an extensive project to help the needy. Even more impressive to me are three important areas that signify their primary involvement. For Andrew, "new medicines"; for Blakey, "hunger" and "poverty."

Need more be said?

PART TWO

FROM ADVENT
TO EASTER

3

Proximate Preparation for a Unique Birth

Gaudete Sunday

Strengthen the weak hands,
*   and make firm the feeble knees.*
Say to those who are of a fearful heart,
*   "Be strong, do not fear!*
Here is your God.
*   He will come with vengeance,*
with terrible recompense.
*   He will come and save you."*
                              —Isa. 35:3–4

Be patient, therefore, beloved, until the coming of the Lord. The farmer waits for the precious crop from the earth, being patient with it until it receives the early and the late rains. You also must be patient. Strengthen your hearts, for the coming of the Lord is near. Beloved, do not grumble against one another, so that you may not be judged. See, the Judge is standing at the doors! As an example of suffering and patience, beloved, take the prophets who spoke in the name of the Lord.

                              —James 5:7–10

When John heard in prison what the Messiah was doing, he sent word by his disciples and said to him, "Are you the one who is to come, or are we to wait for another?" Jesus answered them, "Go and tell John what you hear and see: the blind receive their sight, the lame walk, the lepers are cleansed, the deaf hear, the dead are raised, and the poor have good news brought to them. And blessed is anyone who takes no offense at me."

As they went away, Jesus began to speak to the crowds about John . . . "the one about whom it is written:

> *'See, I am sending my messenger ahead of you,*
> *who will prepare your way before you.'*

Truly I tell you, among those born of women no one has arisen greater than John the Baptist; yet the least in the kingdom of heaven is greater than he."   —Matt. 11:2–7a, 10b–11

Every committed Christian carries a vocabulary. I mean a set of familiar words and phrases that help clarify what "brand" of Christianity he or she follows. Examples? Belief, hope, fear, sacrifice, Mass, Communion, Eucharist, sacred species, holy host, bread and wine, homily.

Not so clear when the central word, the important word, for today's Catholic liturgy is a Latin word: *Gaudete.* This Latin word should make your day. How? Three short points.

I

Advent is a time of waiting. However, *gaudete* asserts that while we wait, we "rejoice." *Gaudete* is equivalent to a command — a command to each of us. Not an invitation or suggestion.

The Lord's coming is announced at the start of Advent. Proclaimed in the entrance antiphon of Gaudete Sunday, the announcement is changed to, "The Lord is near." On this third Sunday of Advent, we rejoice not only in the future coming of the Lord; we rejoice *now* as we welcome the Lord not only to the world at large but also and more intimately into our own hearts. Simply, live with joy.

II

Today is a most appropriate time to examine how we might embrace more fully our joy over the Lord's coming into our lives more completely. So often we equate joy with a kind of energetic exuberance and we forget that even joy requires strength. Isaiah reminds us to ask God to "strengthen . . . weak hands, and make firm . . . feeble knees." Simply, pray for fortitude.

III

James reminds us to be patient until the coming of the Lord. A Dominican friar, Brother Hyacinth Cordell, poignantly ties patience to fortitude through his observation that "patience . . . can be thought of as 'fortitude over time.' "[5] Throughout church history many have viewed Gaudete Sunday in Advent as a parallel to Laetare Sunday in Lent. Both observances are breaks amid solemn seasons offering us, commanding us not only to adore the Lord but to adore him with joy.

Rejuvenated, fortified by our rejoicing, we continue the season of Advent, this season of waiting. But rather than endure a passive period of waiting, let us follow the same mandate that Jesus gave the messengers of John the Baptist: "Go and tell John what you hear and see: the blind receive their sight, the lame walk, the lepers are cleansed, the deaf hear, the dead are raised, and the poor have good news brought to them. And blessed is anyone who takes no offence at me" (Matt. 11:4–5). Indeed, rejoice!

4

Out of the Mouths of Babes

A Homily for Christmas Eve

Good friends in Christ: Today (1) a Christmas story, (2) a reflection on that story, and (3) a suggestion for your story and mine.

I

First, the Christmas story. It was Christmas Eve at famed Riverside Church in New York City, and with William Sloane Coffin Jr. scheduled to preach, the pews were packed. The Christmas pageant was on and had come to the point where the innkeeper was to say there was no room at the inn for Joseph and Mary pregnant with Jesus.

The part seemed perfect for Tim, an earnest youth of the congregation who had Down Syndrome. Only one line to memorize, and he had practiced it again and again with his parents and with the pageant director. He seemed to have mastered it.

So there Tim stood at the altar, a bathrobe over his clothes, as Mary and Joseph made their way down the center aisle. They approached him, said their lines, and waited for his reply. "There's no room at the inn," he boomed out, just as rehearsed. But then, as Mary and Joseph turned to travel further, Tim suddenly yelled, "Wait!" They turned back startled. "You can stay at my house," he called.

Bill Coffin strode to the pulpit, said "Amen," and sat down. It was, as Marian Wright Edelman says, the best sermon he never preached.[6]

II

Second, a reflection on the story. What in young Tim's "You can stay at my house" forced from Bill Coffin's lips that strong "Amen," compelled him to cancel his carefully constructed Christmas sermon? It was not that Tim had preempted what Coffin was about to preach. It was, I suggest, a combination of factors: the spontaneity of Tim's outcry, his quick response to this moment's need (a home for the homeless), a child's caring. All this, and perhaps much else, made Coffin's sermon not unhelpful, only unnecessary.

I doubt that any of those who crowded Riverside Church that Christmas Eve will soon, if ever, forget a boy with Down Syndrome uttering to a homeless Holy Family six memorable monosyllables, "You can stay at my house."

III

Third, a suggestion for your story and mine. In brief, the Riverside Church experience should not become an isolated memory. Similarly for all who, like myself, have only read an account of the pageant. Young Tim's spontaneous outburst, "You can stay at my house," should serve as a stimulus to all of us. A stimulus to live lives of justice.

I mean the justice that runs through so much of Scripture: relationships of love. A justice that Christians find expressed by Jesus in revealing words he will say at the Last Judgment to explain why "the sheep" will "inherit the kingdom":

> "For I was hungry and you gave me food, I was thirsty and you gave me something to drink, I was a stranger and you welcomed me, I was naked and you gave me clothing, I was sick and you took care of me, I was in prison and you visited me.... Truly, I tell you, just as you did it to one of these who are members of my family, you did it for me." (Matt. 25:35–40)

Such, dear friends, is clearly the kind of Christmas giving that delights the heart of Jesus, the Just One, the Righteous One, of the New Testament (e.g., Acts 3:14; 7:52; 22:14).

A Christlike Christmas gift? Give food to a poor family; send clothes, good clothes, to the Salvation Army; welcome ignored immigrants into your home; visit the sick and the lonely; even have the courage to spend time with a man or woman behind bars. The possibilities are numerous. Open your minds, open your hearts, and let Christ inspire your self-giving.

5

A Light, a Star, an Epiphany

Solemnity of the Epiphany

Arise, shine; for your light has come,
*   and the glory of the Lord has risen upon you.*
For darkness shall cover the earth,
*   and thick darkness the peoples;*
but the Lord will arise upon you,
*   and his glory will appear over you.*
Nations shall come to your light,
*   and kings to the brightness of your dawn.*

Lift up your eyes and look around;
*   they all gather together, they come to you;*
your sons shall come from far away,
*   and your daughters shall be carried on their*
*   nurses' arms.*   —Isa. 60:1–4

In the time of King Herod, after Jesus was born in Bethlehem of Judea, wise men from the East came to Jerusalem, asking, "Where is the child who has been born king of the Jews? For we observed his star at its rising, and have come to pay him homage." When King Herod heard this, he was frightened, and all Jerusalem with him. . . . Then Herod secretly called for the wise men and learned from them the exact time when the star had appeared. Then he sent them to Bethlehem, saying, "Go and search diligently for the child; and when you have found him, bring me word so that I may also go and pay him homage." When they had heard the king, they set out; and there, ahead of them, went the star that they had seen at its rising, until it stopped over the place where the child was. When they saw that the star had stopped, they were overwhelmed with joy. On entering the house, they saw the child with Mary his mother; and they knelt down and paid him homage. Then, opening their treasure chests, they offered him gifts of gold, frankincense, and myrrh. And having been warned in a dream not to return to Herod, they left for their own country by another road.

—Matt. 2:1–3a, 7–12

This is the reason that I Paul am a prisoner for Christ Jesus for the sake of you Gentiles—for surely you have already heard of the commission of God's grace that was given to me for you, and how the mystery was made known to me by revelation, as I wrote above in a few words, a reading of which will enable you to perceive my understanding of the mystery of Christ. In former generations this mystery was not made known to humankind, as it has now been revealed to his holy apostles and prophets by the Spirit: that is, the Gentiles have become fellow heirs, members of the same body, and sharers in the promise in Christ Jesus through the gospel.
—Eph. 3:1–6

Today's solemnity of the Epiphany hides a history that is centuries long and complex.[7] But a homily is not a history. A homily is a message, and the message usually takes its cue from the readings in the liturgy. And so shall I proceed. I begin with Isaiah, move on to Matthew, close with apostle Paul.

I

I begin with Isaiah because he opens up for us the meaning of Epiphany. The word derives from a Greek term that means "manifestation." And the manifestation Isaiah foretells has been neatly expressed by biblical scholar Daniel Harrington: "The passage from Isaiah 60 looks forward to a light that will shine forth from Jerusalem. It foresees that all the nations of the world will walk by that light, will acknowledge that light, and so will proclaim the praises of the God of Israel."[8]

II

Turn now to Matthew. Among the evangelists, only Matthew narrates the manifestation of the Messiah to the Magi. Astrologers, they have seen the star that revealed a newborn "king of the Jews" and have come from the East to Jerusalem to pay him homage. Hearing this, King Herod is greatly troubled, frightened. Learning from chief priests and scribes the Messiah's birthplace is Bethlehem, Herod sends the Magi there to "search diligently for the child" and, after finding him, to let the king know, so that he, too, "may go and pay him homage."

The Magi set out and, wonder of wonders, their star precedes them, stops over the house where the child and his mother are. The Magi go in, prostrate themselves, pay the child homage. After offering him their gifts —

gold, frankincense, and myrrh — they leave for home by another route.

An epiphany never to be forgotten, this very first recorded instance of the infant Messiah to non-Jews from the East. And yet, this touching episode in God's plan for our salvation had a tragic byproduct. "When Herod saw that he had been tricked by the wise men, he was infuriated, and he sent and killed all the children in and around Bethlehem who were two years old or under, according to the time that he had learned from the wise men" (Matt. 2:16).

III

I close, briefly, with the apostle Paul. In his Letter to the Ephesians there is a sentence highly pertinent to what Matthew has told us about the Magi. Paul speaks of "the mystery of Christ [which] in former generations . . . was not made known to humankind, as it has now been revealed to his holy apostles and prophets by the Spirit: that is, the Gentiles have become fellow heirs, members of the same body, and sharers in the promise in Christ Jesus through the gospel" (Eph. 3:4b–6).

Of non-Jews, it is not only "wise men" from the East who are included in the Lord's epiphany, in Jesus' self-manifestation. Jesus is the light of the world, for all nations, for all people, for all time. *Today* he is our light.

6

You Will Name Him Jesus

Annunciation of the Lord

Again, the Lord spoke to Ahaz, saying, "Ask for a sign of the Lord your God; let it be deep as Sheol or high as heaven." But Ahaz said, "I will not ask and I will not put the Lord to a test." Then Isaiah said: "Hear then, O house of David! Is it too little for you to weary mortals, that you weary my God also? Therefore the Lord himself will give you a sign: Look, the young woman is with child and shall bear a son, and shall name him Immanuel." —Isa. 7:10–14

In the sixth month, the angel Gabriel was sent by God to a town of Galilee called Nazareth, to a virgin betrothed to a man whose name was Joseph, of the house of David. The virgin's name was Mary. And he came to her and said, "Greetings, favored one! The Lord is with you." ... Mary said to the angel, "How can this be, since I am a virgin?" The angel said to her, "The Holy Spirit will come upon you, and the power of the Most High will overshadow you; therefore the child to be born will be holy; he will be called Son of God. And now, your relative Elizabeth in her old age has also conceived a son; and this is the sixth month for her who was said to be barren. For nothing will be impossible with God." Then Mary said, "Here am I, the servant of the

Lord; let it be with me according to your word." Then the angel departed from her. —Luke 1:26–28, 34–38

On this profound festival with its engrossing readings, time forces me to focus on the Gospel. And here I dwell briefly on (1) the messenger, (2) the message, and (3) Mary's acceptance — inevitably overlapping.

I

The messenger is the angel Gabriel. As Luke has it, Gabriel "was sent by God" to Nazareth with a message for a virgin named Mary. Gabriel came to her and said, "Greetings, favored one! The Lord is with you" (Luke 1:26–28), and delivered God's message.

What manner of "annunciation" was this? Was it, as some scholars suggest, Luke's way of recounting an interior, spiritual experience? What really happened? Replies expert biblicist Joseph A. Fitzmyer, "We shall never know." But he goes on to say, "In this matter the important thing is to attend to the message about the child that is made known."[9] And this is precisely what I proceed to do.

II

The angel's message to Mary is an announcement that presents Jesus and his future in two stages. The first stage in the identification and role of Jesus finds exalted expression in verses 32–33: "He will be great and will be called the Son of the Most High, and the Lord God will give to him the throne of his ancestor David. He will reign over the house of Jacob for ever, and of his kingdom there will be no end."

The second stage (vv. 34–37) carries the identification of Jesus significantly further. This child will be born of a virgin, of Mary. In response to Mary's perplexity on how to reconcile conception of a child with her virginity, Gabriel conveys a remarkable promise: "The Holy Spirit will come upon you, and the power of the Most High will overshadow you; therefore the child to be born will be holy; he will be called Son of God" (v. 35).

On that text, I believe it is important for preachers and their congregations to be aware that, as Fitzmyer states, "The language used here is highly figurative; neither verb, . . . 'come upon' or . . . 'overshadow', has an immediate connotation of conception, let alone a sexual implication. They are figurative expressions of the mysterious intervention of God's Spirit and power that will bring about Jesus' Davidic role and his divine filiation."[10]

III

A third and final word: on Mary's assent and what followed. Her simple yet awesome acquiescence will never depart from us: "Here am I, the servant of the Lord; let it be with me according to your word" (v. 38). Awesome because now the link between heaven and earth in God's plan for our redemption has been forged and the divine is about to become human, God become man. A "yes" to God that would reach from Nazareth to Calvary, where Mary stood beneath a cross and heard her Son murmur, "It is finished."

I cannot end without a brief word on Mary after her assent and newly pregnant with Jesus. "In those days," Luke says all too vaguely, "Mary set out and went with haste to a Judean town in the hill country" (Luke 1:39) to see a relative, Elizabeth, Zechariah's wife. Why "with haste"? Because Gabriel had told Mary that Elizabeth, though aged and called barren, had also conceived a son and was in the sixth month of pregnancy. I feel quite sure that Mary made the trip to congratulate Elizabeth and help her through the final three months. But I suspect that Mary also wanted to share her own joy with Elizabeth; she could hardly have found an interested ear in Nazareth. And you know what happened when Elizabeth heard Mary's greeting: "The child leapt in her womb. And Elizabeth was filled with the Holy Spirit and exclaimed with a loud cry, 'Blessed are you among women, and blessed is the fruit of your womb'" (Luke 1:41–42).

A striking sequence from Gabriel's announcement and Mary's acquiescence: the first meeting of Jesus and John, his precursor and baptizer to come.

7

Joy Even in Lent

Laetare Sunday

So if anyone is in Christ, there is a new creation: everything old has passed away; see, everything has become new! All this is from God, who reconciled us to himself through Christ, and has given us the ministry of reconciliation; that is, in Christ God was reconciling the world to himself, not counting their trespasses against them, and entrusting the message of reconciliation to us. So we are ambassadors for Christ, since God is making his appeal through us; we entreat you on behalf of Christ, be reconciled to God. For our sake he made him to be sin who knew no sin, so that in him we might become the righteousness of God.
— 2 Cor. 5:17–21

When I began this homily, *laetare* ("rejoice") was uppermost in my mind. The clear "break" with Lenten language, the optional use of rose vestments, the "joy" in the Latin subtitle, the parallel with Advent's third Sunday, "Gaudete" ("rejoice!") — all these together may seem to envision a one-day relaxation from the rigors of Lent. Not quite. Lent remains, but at its very heart the liturgy pauses to give us an anticipation of resurrection. To grasp this, we go back to the Scripture for glimpses of God's generosity, of a father's fidelity.

I

First, to the Old Testament. The biblical book of Joshua, the successor of Moses, is important here. For "the purpose of the book is to demonstrate God's fidelity in giving to the Israelites the land he had promised them for an inheritance."[11] The "promised land" is, of course, the covenant the Lord made with Abram, saying: "To your descendants I give this land, from the river of Egypt to the great river, the river Euphrates, the land of the Kenites, the Kenizzites, the Kadmonites, the Hittites, the Perizzites, the Rephaim, the Amorites, the Canaanites, the Girgashites, and the Jebusites" (Gen. 15:18b–21).

II

Second, to Paul's second letter to Corinth's Christians. "So if anyone is in Christ, there is a new creation: everything old has passed away; see, everything has become new! All this is from God, who reconciled us to himself through Christ. . . . God was reconciling the world to himself, not counting their trespasses against them. . . . For our sake he made him to be sin who knew no sin, so that in him we might become the righteousness of God" (2 Cor. 5:17–21).

Once again, in the very middle of Lent, absorbed by a Christ with eyes fixed on Calvary, I am subtly but clearly reminded that I trudge through these forty days as a risen Christian. I dare not pretend, even beneath the cross, that Jesus has not yet risen.

III

Third, to a parable. The problem (relaxation or anticipation?) reaches a new level in Luke with the parable of the Lost Son. The story is familiar to you, but let me tell it with some of my own words.

The younger of two sons asks and receives his inheritance from his father. With all his belongings he sets off to a far country, where he dissipates his inheritance. Hit by famine, he tends swine, does not get their food to eat, is dying of hunger.

Resolved to return home and confess his sinful past, he will ask his father to treat him like one of his hired workers.

As he approaches home, his father sees him. Full of compassion, he rushes to embrace and kiss him. In the home he orders for his son the finest robe, a ring, and sandals, topped off by a celebratory feast. The older son is angry, refuses to enter the house and share in the music. He has served his father "all these years," never disobeyed his orders. No party for him, only for the son who swallowed up his father's property with prostitutes. The father's response is classic — every word: "Son, you are always with me, and all that is mine is yours. But we had to celebrate and rejoice, because this brother of yours was dead and has come to life; he was lost and has been found" (Luke 15:31–32).

Hardly a Gospel for a traditional Lenten day. If we focus on the happy outburst of the father in the Gospel that his son has come from death to life, as well as his excited insistence on celebration and joy — our *Laetare* this day could easily extend to an empty tomb.

8

Every Day a Holy Thursday

Holy Thursday

For I received from the Lord what I also handed on to you, that the Lord Jesus on the night when he was betrayed took a loaf of bread, and when he had given thanks, he broke it and said, "This is my body that is for you. Do this in remembrance of me." In the same way he took the cup also, after supper, saying, "This cup is the new covenant in my blood. Do this, as often as you drink it, in remembrance of me." For as often as you eat this bread and drink the cup, you proclaim the Lord's death until he comes. — 1 Cor. 11:23–26

"Those who eat my flesh and drink my blood abide in me, and I in them. Just as the living Father sent me, and I live because of the Father, so whoever eats me will live because of me. This is the bread that came down from heaven, not like that which your ancestors ate, and they died. But the one who eats this bread will live for ever." — John 6:56–58

The first Holy Thursday raised two challenges. The first challenge came to Jesus, the second to his apostles. The challenge to Jesus? He had to go, and he wanted to stay. On the morrow he would have to leave the apostles; it was his Father's will. But never had he loved his favorite friends as dearly as at this supper. How could he possibly leave them?

Jesus' solution? He will go, and he will stay; he will leave us, and he will remain with us. He will take from his disciples, from us, the sensory charm of his presence. No longer will his friends hear the music and thunder of his voice, sense the fascination of his smile, or be touched by his tears. And still he will stay, will leave with us the reality, the truth, of that presence.

How? Jesus took bread, blessed it, and gave it to his disciples saying, "Take, eat; this is my body"; then the cup, "Drink from it, all of you; for this is my blood of the covenant" (Matt. 26:26–28). In the Eucharist the Jesus of Palestine indeed remains with us. Not only a real presence, but the realization of Jesus' startling promise some months earlier, "Whoever eats me will live because of me" (John 6:57).

Move now to Holy Thursday's second challenge, the challenge to the apostles. Jesus rose from the table, took off his robe, tied a towel around his waist, and washed the feet of the Twelve. Only Peter, as usual, protested. But surely all were surprised, even embarrassed; for it was an act that could not be required of the lowest Jewish slave.

Back at the table, Jesus challenged his disciples: "You call me Teacher and Lord — and you are right, for that is what I am. So if I . . . have washed your feet, you also ought to wash one another's feet. For I have set you an example, that you also should do as I have done to you" (John 13:13–15). The challenge is to be *men for others*.

All of which leads neatly to you and me. The same two challenges: Eucharist and footwashing. A subtle peril lurks in daily Communion — the peril that haunts almost anything we experience time and time again — within clergy or laity, in the pulpit or at a desk job. Early on, sheer delight; with time, mere routine. We must try to recapture every so often the glow that lights up a first Communion, the Communion at an ordination, or the Communion at a wedding.

But our Eucharist is not a private party, a "me and Jesus" experience. The Jesus who told his disciples "This is my body which is given for you" (Luke 22:19) told the same disciples that they must wash one another's feet. The same Jesus gives you and me his body and blood, soul and divinity, and insists that we be men and women in service to others, loving as he loves.

Yes, Communion and compassion go together, not only on Holy Thursday but every day. Happily, I find this commitment to service in the residents and staff here at Manresa: the Christlike caring for each other evidenced in the work of the staff and the mutual help we Jesuits give to one another. Christ is alive among us every time someone reads a menu to me, a chef prepares a simple lunch or a festive dinner, a Jesuit pushes another man's wheelchair, or a nurse dispenses medication both with competence and humor. These simple yet important moments of service make every day here at Manresa a Holy Thursday, the Eucharistic Christ living within us, the Servant Christ serving with us.

9

Let This Cup Pass?

Holy Thursday

He came out and went, as was his custom, to the Mount of Olives; and the disciples followed him. When he reached the place, he said to them, "Pray that you may not come into the time of trial." Then he withdrew from them about a stone's throw, knelt down, and prayed, "Father, if you are willing, remove this cup from me; yet, not my will but yours be done." Then an angel from heaven appeared to him and gave him strength. In his anguish he prayed more earnestly, and his sweat became like great drops of blood falling down on the ground.

—Luke 22:39–44

Last year on this same festal day I preached here at Manresa on two unique events of the first Holy Thursday: Jesus instituting the Eucharist and washing the feet of the Twelve.

But Holy Thursday did not end there. When Jesus and the disciples left the upper room, their destination was Gethsemane, an olive orchard on the western slope of Jesus' beloved Mount of Olives (Matthew, Mark, and Luke simply say "Gethsemane," John calls it a "garden"). Joining Jesus in his garden, let's listen to his prayer, discover his Father's response, and end with a prayerful reflection on our own garden.

I

First, the prayer of Jesus. He has just confessed to Peter, James, and John, "I am deeply grieved, even to death; remain here, and stay awake with me" (Matt. 26:38). Moving a bit away, he falls prostrate and prays, "My Father, if it is possible, let this cup pass from me; yet, not what I want but what you want" (v. 39). And a little later, with a slight change in emphasis, "If this [cup] cannot pass unless I drink it, your will be done" (v. 42).

Obvious in this prayer is Jesus' total submission to the will of his Father. And yet, more striking to me is how utterly human his prayer reveals him to be. He is well aware that he is about to be arrested, that a cruel death will follow. But for this he took our flesh; for this he lived. This death he predicted time and again. When Peter protested that nothing like this should ever happen to his Master, Jesus turned on him almost fiercely, "Get behind me, Satan!" And still, at this critical hour in Gethsemane's garden, something deep in his humanity cries out to his Father, "Don't let me die!"

II

Second, the response to Jesus' prayer. Only one response is recorded, two verses — verses I suspect many of you may remember: "Then an angel from heaven appeared to him and gave him strength. In his anguish he prayed more earnestly, and his sweat became like great drops of blood falling down on the ground" (Luke 22:43–44).

The verses reveal a response to the prayer of Jesus and make clear why this visit of Jesus to the garden in Gethsemane is often termed his agony. On the other hand, it is important for preachers of the Word to know that among the four evangelists it is only in Luke that we find these two verses. Because they are absent from the oldest Lucan papyrus manuscripts, there is serious conflict among biblical scholars as to whether these verses can be traced back to the authentic Luke.[12]

III

Third, a reflection on our own garden. I find it fascinating that Manresa has much in common with Gethsemane. Like Jesus, we have not come to our garden to die. Oh yes, Jesus knew he would be arrested in the garden that night and condemned on the morrow. But it was not to be arrested that he came to the garden. Gethsemane was a favorite of his for prayer; here he would pray in agony to his Father, "Don't let me die!"

Similarly for you and me here at Manresa. It is not primarily because our catalog[13] proclaims most of us are "praying for the Church and the Society" that our collective presence makes this garden a privileged place of prayer. Our prayer lives are far broader. They include our aches and agonies, our fears and frustrations, even loneliness, all offered to God for the hungry, the hopeless, and so many others in need — such is the wide scope of prayer in our Manresa garden.

Happily, the scope of Manresan prayer does not prevent us from echoing on occasion the plea of Jesus to his Father: "If it is possible, let this cup pass from me."

10

For Me?

Good Friday

When you make his life an offering for sin,
  he shall see his offspring, and shall prolong his days;
through him the will of the Lord shall prosper.
  Out of his anguish he shall see light;
he shall find satisfaction through his knowledge.
  The righteous one, my servant, shall make many righteous,
  and he shall bear their iniquities.
Therefore I will allot him a portion with the great,
  and he shall divide the spoil with the strong;
because he poured out himself to death,
  and was numbered with the transgressors;
yet he bore the sin of many,
  and made intercession for the transgressors.
  —Isa. 53:10b–12

One of the criminals who were hanged there kept deriding him and saying, "Are you not the Messiah? Save yourself and us!" But the other rebuked him, saying, "Do you not fear God, since you are under the same sentence of condemnation? And we indeed have been condemned justly, for we are getting what we deserve for our deeds, but this man has done nothing wrong."

Then he said, "Jesus, remember me when you come into your kingdom." He replied, "Truly I tell you, today you will be with me in Paradise."   — Luke 23:39–43

During my early years as a priest, Good Friday afternoon was often the time for a set of seven sermons on the seven last "words" of Jesus from the cross. But this particular situation permits me only a single sermon. My selection? A sermon with a title in two monosyllables: "For Me?" Three stages in its development: (1) Jesus was born for me, (2) Jesus lived for me, (3) Jesus died for me.

I

The first stage we discover in the little town of Bethlehem. There, in a shelter adjacent to a crowded inn, a young woman named Mary, the wife of Joseph, gave birth to a male child. The child, soon to be named Jesus, was the unique divine Son of God the Father.

The child, we know, was born "for us" to offer salvation to every human from the first Adam to the last Anti-Christ. I urge you, however, to get used to thinking and saying "Jesus was born *for me*." It might keep you from seeing Bethlehem from a distance — Jesus born for a vast but passing "world."

II

Similarly for stage two. In theological theory little Bethlehem could have sufficed for our salvation. But a far-seeing Trinity had much more in mind. Not only would Jesus be born as we are born; he would live much as we live. He would walk and talk, smile and weep, eat and drink, tire and sleep. Not because he had to; only because he wanted to share our life as much as possible. And, of course, because he wanted his humanity to stimulate our activity: his obedience to Joseph and Mary in Nazareth, his compliance with his Father's will, his recourse to prayer, his impatience with injustice, and so much more. "All this" each of you can say, "All this for me."

III

The third stage tops all else: Jesus died for me. True, Jesus died for all that is human, for humankind, but not in some form of gigantic block. Each of us here is as well known to Jesus as was the crucified thief whom he promised from his own cross, "Truly I tell you, today you will be with me in Paradise" (Luke 23:43). And still he died for every one of us. Died not only for eleven faithful apostles but for Judas as well. Not for his mother alone but for the woman hustled before him for adultery.

His death? Jesus did not have to die. The divine plan for transforming humankind from sin to sanctity through the Son of God in our flesh did indeed transpire through the violent death he predicted. And some may argue that a more normal death clearly offered for our salvation could have achieved the remarkable results for which he was born and lived — and perhaps without the misunderstandings and disagreements that time and again plague Jews and Christians.

And yet, was not his crucifixion so central to Jesus' vision of redemption till the end of time, so essential a symbol of love divine and human, that its negatives must be overcome or disregarded? The crucifixion transcends everything!

11

Hope for the Hopeless?

An Easter Homily

Then Peter began to speak to them: "I truly understand that God shows no partiality, but in every nation anyone who fears him and does what is right is acceptable to him. You know the message he sent to the people of Israel, preaching peace by Jesus Christ — he is Lord of all. That message spread throughout Judea, beginning in Galilee after the baptism that John announced: how God anointed Jesus of Nazareth with the Holy Spirit and with power; how he went about doing good and healing all who were oppressed by the devil, for God was with him. We are witnesses to all that he did both in Judea and in Jerusalem. They put him to death by hanging him on a tree."

— Acts 10:34–39

Now on that same day two of them were going to a village called Emmaus, about seven miles from Jerusalem, and talking with each other about all these things that had happened. While they were talking and discussing, Jesus himself came near and went with them, but their eyes were kept from recognizing him. And he said to them, "What are you discussing with each other while you walk along? . . ." He asked them, "What things?" They replied, "The things about Jesus of Nazareth, who was a prophet mighty in deed and word before God and all the people, and how our chief priests and leaders handed him over to be condemned to death and crucified him. But we had hoped that he was the one to redeem Israel. Yes, and besides all this, it is now the third day since these things took place. Moreover, some women of our group astounded us. They were at the tomb early this morning, and when they did not find his body there, they came back and told us that they had indeed seen a vision of angels who said that he was alive."   —Luke 24:13–23

"We were hoping." A phrase, a frustration that has haunted me Easter after Easter. A wistful wish uttered by two disciples to a risen Jesus they did not recognize. "We had hoped that he was the one to redeem Israel" (Luke 24:21). "We had hoped"—till he died.

The experience of the two disciples raises three important questions for preacher and congregation. (1) A question too vast to answer fully: How extensive are the hopeless? (2) How describe Easter hope? (3) How effective might Easter hope be on the hopeless?

I

Hopeless are uncounted numbers: those who have given up all expectation for a better tomorrow and those who have never had such expectation. I am thinking of the more than nine million men, women, and children who perish from hunger each year. I am mourning the fifteen million children around the globe orphaned to AIDS. I am remembering the reality of nearly four hundred thousand homeless veterans living on the streets during any given year. I am agonizing over the far too many who lost their homes — and some their entire family — in the unrelenting waters of Katrina or the southeast Asia tsunami. At ninety-three, I am keenly empathizing with the elderly who do not live in community and those of all ages who are uninsured and at the mercy, if not the whimsy, of the remarkably few who control access to medical services and grossly overpriced medications.

If you need an example painfully close to your experience and mine, hear Bob Herbert in the *New York Times:* "Black American males inhabit a universe in which joblessness is frequently the norm, where the idea of getting up each morning and going off to work can seem stranger to a lot of them than the dream of hitting the lottery, where the dignity that comes from supporting oneself and one's family has too often been replaced by a numbing sense of hopelessness."[14]

II

Against this backdrop of contemporary hopelessness, what is Easter hope? Of highest importance is the promise of eternal life — intimate life with God now and forever. As Jesus phrased it, "This is eternal life, that they may know you, the only true God, and Jesus Christ whom you have sent" (John 17:3).

In Christian living, hope cannot be limited to *knowing and loving God* in this world or the next. It includes what we request in the Lord's Prayer — "our daily bread" (the Eucharist?), God's will in our day-to-day activity, forgiven and forgiving, graced to avoid evil. It also encompasses our duties to one another and to the earth.

And still, Easter hope is compatible with suffering, with a respectable poverty, with failures, with all sorts of human ills. But Easter hope is impossible to sustain when God is no longer part of the equation. A natural hope is not to be despised; unnumbered humans live their lives on it. Even Christians day after day live on natural hopes of good things to come: sunny weather, satisfying work, a happy marriage, a graceful aging. And still the hope surpassing all others must be the Easter expectation: life lived in endless love with our God whose very name is Love.

III

How effective might Easter hope be on the hopeless? The answer, I suggest, depends in large measure on the cooperation that concerned Christian individuals and communities seek and obtain from governments, health care groups, such organizations as the Children's Defense Fund, or any of the centers for peace or justice or environment.

One example: Venezuela, over a period of five years. Several of the poorest barrios were dramatically transformed. As an American observer put it, "The revolution has included literacy classes, the formation of small agrarian and industrial cooperatives, clean water and improved sanitary conditions, and free medical services. Their spirit of enthusiasm and hope filled the air."[15] Little wonder, for the country's Constitution, framed in part by the people and passed by popular referendum, is strikingly akin to Catholic social teaching.

An inspiration, I should hope (yes, hope), to all believers in our country to strain together to gift or restore natural hope to the homeless and the hungry, the fearful and the forgotten, the lonely and the unloved — any and all who see no reason for awakening to a tomorrow. Once enlivened in flesh and spirit by believers such as you, they will be ready to receive Easter joy: the grace to know and love God each hour here below and the promise of life with God for all eternity.

PART THREE

SPECIAL FEASTS AND MEMORIALS

12

Receive the Holy Spirit

Pentecost Sunday

When the day of Pentecost had come, they were all together in one place. And suddenly from heaven there came a sound like the rush of a violent wind, and it filled the entire house where they were sitting. Divided tongues, as of fire, appeared among them, and a tongue rested on each of them. All of them were filled with the Holy Spirit and began to speak in other languages, as the Spirit gave them ability. Now there were devout Jews from every nation under heaven living in Jerusalem ... [yet] in our own languages we hear them speaking about God's deed of power. — Acts 2:1–5, 11*

Now there are varieties of gifts, but the same Spirit; and there are varieties of services, but the same Lord; and there are varieties of activities, but it is the same God who activates all of them in everyone.... For just as the body is one and has many members, and all the members of the body, though many, are one body, so it is with Christ. For in the one Spirit we were all baptized into one body — Jews or Greeks, slaves or free — and we were all made to drink of one Spirit.

— 1 Cor. 12:4–6, 12–13*

When it was evening on that day, the first day of the week, and the doors of the house where the disciples had met were locked for fear of the Jews, Jesus came and stood among them and said, "Peace be with you." After he said this, he showed them his hands and his side. Then the disciples rejoiced when they saw the Lord. Jesus said to them again, "Peace be with you. As the Father has sent me, so I send you." When he had said this, he breathed on them and said to them, "Receive the Holy Spirit. If you forgive the sins of any, they are forgiven them; if you retain the sins of any, they are retained."   —John 20:19–23

Brothers and sisters: Today's Solemnity of Pentecost brings to an end the Easter season. It does so on a highly positive note: a strong stress on the Holy Spirit. Since the full history of Pentecost, for all its value and interest, is too complex for a homily, I shall (1) focus on Luke's Pentecost story, (2) touch insights from Paul and John on the Holy Spirit, and (3) close with reflections on the significance of Pentecost for our life here at Manresa.

I

There are several startling aspects to Pentecost as described by Luke in Acts 2:1–11. First, Pentecost was celebrated in Jerusalem not only by the apostles. It was being celebrated in Jerusalem as the Feast of Weeks (seven weeks after the second day of Passover) by "Jews from every nation under heaven" (v. 5).

Second, on that Pentecost all the apostles, gathered in one place, were filled with the Holy Spirit and began to speak in other languages as "the Spirit gave them ability"

(v. 4). And, therefore, each Jew and every proselyte in the vast throng sojourning in Jerusalem heard the speaker in the language in which he was brought up.

Third, this Pentecost was most memorable because, as biblical scholar Joseph A. Fitzmyer, S.J., declared, "It was the first opportunity that the Twelve had to confront the twelve tribes of Israel in an official capacity and bear testimony to the risen Christ, having received the power from on high to do so."[16]

Fourth, the confrontation with the tribes, the testimony to the risen Christ, follow swiftly (Acts 2:14–36). When Peter stands up to speak, he addresses "Men of Judea and all who live in Jerusalem" (v. 14). It is "the first recorded sermon of the Christian church."[17] Brief, not an invitation to dialogue. It is an out-and-out challenge: "God has made Jesus both Lord and Messiah." A Peter courageous (needlessly bold?) unto his final words: "this Jesus whom you crucified" (v. 36).

II

Move now to Paul and John, impressive this day for the space they allot to the Holy Spirit. In the second reading we heard Paul enrich the minds and swell the hearts of Corinth's Catholics. How? By revealing the "varieties of gifts . . . from the same Spirit," for example, wisdom, knowledge, faith, healing, prophecy (see 1 Cor. 12:4–11).

Paul also assured the Christians of Rome: "If the Spirit of him who raised Jesus from the dead dwells in you, he who raised Christ from the dead will give life to your mortal bodies also through his Spirit that dwells in you" (Rom. 8:11).

In John's Gospel we heard the risen Jesus say to eleven apostles, "Receive the Holy Spirit" (John 20:22), seemingly for the forgiveness of sins. But in the alternative Gospel text recommended for today John's Jesus is more expressive about the role of the Spirit in our lives: "If you love me, you will keep my commandments. And I will ask the Father, and he will give you another Advocate, to be with you forever. This is the Spirit of truth, whom the world cannot receive, because it neither sees him nor knows him. You know him, because he abides with you, and he will be in you" (John 14:15–17). And shortly afterward: "The Advocate, the Holy Spirit, whom the Father will send in my name, will teach you everything and remind you of all that I have said to you" (v. 26).

III

All well and good, but how might Pentecost be of service to us here at Manresa not only on this day but often throughout the year? I recommend a more intimate relationship with the Holy Spirit. What would that involve? A deeper understanding of the role the Holy Spirit plays in our lives, and a realistic love for the Holy Spirit that rivals the love we have for God the Father and for His Son in our flesh.

It makes sense. After all, that divine Spirit, the Third Person of the Trinity, is at this moment alive within us, active within us, the reason we can say, "Jesus is Lord," the Power behind so many of the good actions we take for granted. So then, why not use this Pentecost to revitalize our friendship with the Holy Spirit? A brief apology might be in order. But, as we New Yorkers say, "Not to worry!" The Spirit's patience has a long and generous history.

All I am struggling to say about "men of Manresa" and the Holy Spirit has been neatly summed up by Jesuit Scripture scholar Daniel J. Harrington:

> The Advocate's task will be to teach the followers of Jesus everything they need to know and to remind them of the words of Jesus. The Advocate is to be the "stand-in" or representative of the earthly Jesus. What would allow the disciples to carry on from the earthly Jesus and bring his word to others was the gift of the Holy Spirit. But to be instructed by the Advocate it is necessary first of all to be open to the Holy Spirit. That involves recognizing that God may have surprises in store for us as individuals and as a community of faith.[18]

13

The Birth of John the Baptist

John Associated with Jesus Always

When [God] had removed [Saul], he made David their king. In his testimony about him he said, "I have found David, son of Jesse, to be a man after my heart, who will carry out all my wishes." Of this man's posterity God has brought to Israel a Savior, Jesus, as he promised; before his coming John had already proclaimed a baptism of repentance to all the people of Israel. And as John was finishing his work, he said, "What do you suppose that I am? I am not he. No, but one is coming after me; I am not worthy to untie the thong of the sandals on his feet." — Acts 13:22–25

"I baptize you with water for repentance, but one who is more powerful than I is coming after me; I am not worthy to carry his sandals. He will baptize you with the Holy Spirit and fire. His winnowing fork is in his hand, and he will clear his threshing floor and will gather his wheat into the granary; but the chaff he will burn with unquenchable fire." — Matt. 3:11–12

I

It is not easy, perhaps not possible, to preach a simplified John the Baptist. Let me focus on what I consider the center of his life and ministry. This I find splendidly expressed in an article on John by Carl R. Kazmierski in the *Modern Catholic Encyclopedia*. Grateful to its scholarly author, I borrow the following as my first major point. Listen to it with uncommon care.

> It is surely significant that, in the New Testament, the ministry of John is always associated with that of Jesus. While the tradition uses a number of different models or images to describe John, nowhere does he stand alone or apart from Jesus and the gospel of the church. John is the one who prepares for, reveals, gives witness to, and even inaugurates its proclamation. With all its diversity, this portrait of John can provide us with access to the process of discernment which begins with the remembrance of his prophetic activity in the wilderness of Judea and culminates in the Fourth Gospel's portrayal of the Baptist as a witness to its own Christology. At the same time, it invites us to hear his call for repentance and to respond as did his own contemporaries and those in the early Church who took up his challenge.[19]

II

Some preachers may find that striking summary of this unique union so closely knitted that its force is not grasped. Several concrete examples will illustrate the association of the ministries of John and Jesus:

1. I see something like a prediction of this association in the gracious visit of Mary pregnant with Jesus to her kinswoman Elizabeth pregnant with John. Recall Elizabeth's joyous welcome: "For as soon as I heard the sound of your greeting, the child in my womb leaped for joy" (Luke 1:44).

2. Now focus on the preoccupation in the preaching of the Baptist. To the Pharisees and Sadducees who came to him to be baptized:

   > "You brood of vipers! Who warned you to flee from the wrath to come? Bear fruit worthy of repentance. Do not presume to say to yourselves, 'We have Abraham as our ancestor'; for I tell you, God is able from these stones to raise up children to Abraham. Even now the axe is lying at the root of the trees; every tree therefore that does not bear good fruit is cut down and thrown into the fire.
   >
   > "I baptize you with water for repentance, but one who is more powerful than I is coming after me; I am not worthy to carry his sandals. He will baptize you with the Holy Spirit and fire. His winnowing fork is in his hand, and he will clear his threshing floor and will gather his wheat into the granary; but the chaff he will burn with unquenchable fire." (Matt. 3:7b–12)

3. Now turn to John's associate in ministry, Jesus. A strikingly similar "sermon point" attracts us later in Matthew: Jesus' strong denunciation of the scribes

and Pharisees to his disciples and the crowds. In shortened form:

> The scribes and the Pharisees have taken their seat on the chair of Moses. Observe what they tell you, but do not follow their example. For they do not practice what they preach. They tie up heavy burdens and lay them on people's shoulders, but they will not lift a finger to remove them. . . . They clean the outside of cup and dish, but inside they are full of greed and self-indulgence. On the outside they appear righteous, but inside they are filled with hypocrisy and lawlessness. (Matt. 23:2–4, 25)

John the Baptist and Jesus the Savior, two incomparable associates in ministry who still today continue to challenge us. Read them, ponder them — live them!

14

Ignatius for Today

Feast of St. Ignatius of Loyola

*Whether you eat or drink, or whatever you do, do everything
for the glory of God. Give no offense to Jews or to Greeks or
to the church of God, just as I try to please everyone in everything I do, not seeking my own advantage but that of many, so
that they may be saved. Be imitators of me, as I am of Christ.*
— 1 Cor. 10:31—11:1

*He put before them another parable: "The kingdom of heaven
is like a mustard seed that someone took and sowed in his field;
it is the smallest of all the seeds, but when it has grown it is the
greatest of shrubs and becomes a tree, so that the birds of the
air come and make nests in its branches."*
— Matt. 13:31–32

Four centuries and a half have fled since St. Ignatius Loyola
ended his life on earth. A significant question: How can we
relate essential aspects of Ignatius's spirituality to today's
Jesuits and our collaborators? In a brief homily I must limit
myself to a single inspiration of Ignatius — perhaps the
most basic of all. I mean his insistence that we constantly
pray for a threefold grace: to "see Jesus more clearly, love

him more dearly, and follow him more nearly." A word on each of these graces.

First, the grace to see Jesus more clearly. Here we are functioning in the area of knowledge; we seek to know. But the knowledge in question here is not the grasping of ideas or facts — the way a Scripture scholar, for example, would know more and more *about* Jesus. No, Ignatius is speaking of an intimate familiarity with Jesus — the way I knew my father, my mother, my brother, Eddie.

Rather than lose you in abstractions, I offer you a well-known example from Ignatius's own life. When the pilgrim Ignatius was about to leave the Holy Land, he wanted to be close to Jesus once again by going back to visit the places where Jesus had walked and prayed. And so he went to the Mount of Olives, to see the stone from which Jesus rose into heaven — a stone on which his footprints are said to be still visible. A touchingly humorous footnote: To see the stone, Ignatius had to bribe guards with a pair of scissors!

And yet, for all his stress on *knowing* Jesus, Ignatius was acutely aware that in a Christian vision knowledge is not an end in itself. At its best it is a step toward love. That love is splendidly apparent in the contemplation that closes the Spiritual Exercises, sometimes titled, "Learning to Love Like God." Genuine love between persons, Ignatius declares, demands an interchange, a giving on both sides. On Jesus' part, the gifts of love are well known and breathtaking: redeeming humankind from sin and death by dying on a cross, shedding divine grace ceaselessly across the world, giving his total self to us in the Eucharist. Our part in the mutual loving is neatly captured by Ignatius in a prayer familiar to Jesuits down the ages:

Take, O Lord, and receive all my liberty, my memory, my understanding, and all my will, whatsoever I have and possess. All these you have given to me; to you, O Lord, I return them all. All are yours; dispose of them all according to your will. Give me your love and your grace, for this is enough for me.

Finally, if we are to follow Jesus more nearly, our love dare not be imprisoned; it must reach out to others. Such was the love of Jesus, from Bethlehem to Calvary. Such was the love of Ignatius, from Manresa (Spain) to Rome. Such must be our love, Jesuits and laity. For to follow Jesus is not to imitate his talk or mimic his walk. To follow Jesus is to be a disciple of Jesus. And a disciple of Jesus not only knows his mind and obeys his will, but communicates his love to others.

Good friends all: Ignatius Loyola is not a saint-for-a-day, to be honored on July 31 and then a mere memory. One way to keep him alive is to start each day with his strong recommendation: ask for the grace to see Jesus more clearly, to love him more dearly, and to follow him more nearly.

15

Sanctity Yesterday,
Sanctity Today

Feast of All Saints

See what love the Father has given us, that we should be called children of God; and that is what we are. The reason the world does not know us is that it did not know him. Beloved, we are God's children now; what we will be has not yet been revealed. What we do know is this: when he is revealed, we will be like him, for we will see him as he is. And all who have this hope in him purify themselves, just as he is pure. — 1 John 3:1–3

When Jesus saw the crowds, he went up the mountain; and after he sat down, his disciples came to him. Then he began to speak, and taught them, saying:

"Blessed are the poor in spirit, for theirs is the kingdom of heaven.

"Blessed are those who mourn, for they will be comforted.

"Blessed are the meek, for they will inherit the earth.

"Blessed are those who hunger and thirst for righteousness, for they will be filled." — Matt. 5:1–6

Almost forty-five years ago I completed serious research on the saints with the publication of *Saints and Sanctity*.[20] The book was born of a problem in contemporary spirituality: What is the significance of yesterday's saint for today's Christian? The question is as relevant now as it was then.

Our question: What significance does yesterday's saint have for today's Christian? What meaning has the sanctity of the past for the holiness of the present? On broad lines, three solutions may be suggested. One extreme insists that usually the lives of the saints are normative for us; the other extreme affirms that the lives of the saints have little or nothing to say to contemporary man or woman; their experiences were too different. The position I have learned to take is a *via media,* an effort to harmonize and unify what is valid. The lives of the saints, or aspects of their lives, or individual episodes in their lives, even legends surrounding saints who did or did not exist illustrate in striking fashion certain principles or facets of Christian spirituality that are permanently valid, that have a relevance transcending persons and places, eras and situations. And even where saintly actions seem embarrassingly eccentric or bizarre, they often lend credence to G. K. Chesterton's contention: "A saint is one who exaggerates what the world and the church have forgotten."[21]

To clarify this, two separate segments are necessary. Recall several saints and spiritualities that, though conceived and born in the distant past, have only grown and increased in influence through centuries.

From the perspective of seventy-five years as a Jesuit let me focus on St. Ignatius Loyola and his *Spiritual Exercises.* Five centuries and more have fled, and Ignatian spirituality now thrives not only among Jesuits but also increasingly among lay Catholics.

How describe the *Spiritual Exercises?* The *Exercises,* one of the classics of Christian spirituality, contains instructions, meditations, and other practices. The first week focuses on sin and its consequences; the second, on the kingdom of God; the third, on the Passion; the fourth, on the risen Christ. The meditations appeal to the retreatant's sense impressions, imagination, and understanding in a way calculated to move him or her toward a decision in the pursuit of perfection. To make the Exercises is to contemplate the mystery of salvation and to discover therein God's will for oneself.

Centuries old but as fresh as today. That's the meaning past sanctity has for present holiness.

PART FOUR

CELEBRATIONS

16

The Gift of Love
for One Another
The Mass for Family and Friends

Is not this the fast that I choose:
   to loose the bonds of injustice,
   to undo the thongs of the yoke,
to let the oppressed go free,
   and to break every yoke?
Is it not to share your bread with the hungry,
   and bring the homeless poor into your house;
when you see the naked, to cover them,
   and not to hide yourself from your own kin?
Then your light shall break forth like the dawn,
   and your healing shall spring up quickly.
               —Isa. 58:6–8a

We know that we have passed from death to life because we love one another. Whoever does not love abides in death. All who hate a brother or sister are murderers, and you know that murderers do not have eternal life abiding in them. We know love by this, that he laid down his life for us—and we ought to lay down our lives for one another. How does God's love abide

89

in anyone who has the world's goods and sees a brother or sister
in need and yet refuses help?

   Little children, let us love, not in word or speech, but in
truth and action.   — 1 John 3:14–18

As we gather this afternoon for Mass, we are uncommonly
fortunate: we may choose from a number of different
Masses. What Mass have we selected? Fittingly, the Mass
for Family and Friends. From this Mass I shall focus on
(1) the opening prayer, (2) the Epistle, and (3) a piece of
pertinent genealogy from the Gospel of Matthew.

I

First, the opening prayer. A powerful prayer, worth repeat-
ing and worth pondering. "Father, by the power of your
Spirit you have filled the hearts of your faithful people with
gifts of love for one another. Hear the prayers we offer for
our relatives and friends. Give them health of mind and
body that they may do your will with perfect love."

   The prayer begins with a fact: our love of one another.
That love, we are told, is a gift of the Holy Spirit — therefore not simply something we humans create on our own.
Then we ask our Father in heaven to give our family and
our friends mental and bodily health. Why? Not just to
feel good. No, to be able to do with perfect love whatever
God asks of us.

II

Second, the passages from the First Letter of John. Here
we look more deeply into the opening prayer's gift of

love — our love for one another, for family and friends. How have we come to know what that sort of love is like? By focusing on the Christ who laid down his life for us.

Yes, strange as it may sound, perhaps excessive, Christian love at its best involves a readiness to sacrifice life itself for others.

The most obvious examples of such self-sacrifice are the thousands of martyrs down through the ages, from the first Christian martyr Stephen to the four American church-women savagely murdered some years ago in El Salvador. But not to be forgotten are the countless men and women who, in the footsteps of Mother Teresa of Calcutta and Jesuit Horace McKenna of Washington, D.C., give themselves so utterly to the poor and the oppressed that their lives can be called bloodless martyrdom.

This leads concretely to what the First Letter of John calls our brothers and sisters "in need." I mean our hungry children, our underpaid fathers, our penniless widows, war veterans on our city streets, the AIDS-afflicted, the lonely, the immigrants, the imprisoned — the list is long and the numbers are growing.

How respond? At times Scripture is painfully blunt. Jesus tells us: feed the hungry, clothe the naked, house the homeless, visit the sick and the shackled (see Matt. 25:31–46). Nor does he only talk it; in a desert he really feeds five thousand hungry folk. Such words and actions from Jesus recall time and again a declaration by God on the lips of the prophet Isaiah: "...this [is the] fast that I choose: to loose the bonds of injustice,...to let the oppressed go free,...to share your bread with the hungry, and bring the homeless poor into your house; when you see the naked, to cover them, and not to hide yourself from your own kin" (Isa. 58:6–7).

Do not turn your back on your own flesh! A striking injunction, making clear beyond question how incredibly close each human is to every other. The unending problem is how to live what we are.

III

Third, the evangelist Matthew. How does he fit into our picture? Genealogists point to an intriguing parallel: the Old Testament begins with creation; the New Testament begins with genealogy. A genealogy of Jesus starting with Abraham, the father of Israel. A family tree in detail: forty-two generations. Why tell this here? Because the eye-capturing position Matthew allots to the genealogy suggests to me how important it is, how exciting it can be, for each living family member to know the family's roots, to hear the family stories, to trade experiences. In this way, I believe, we can deepen and expand the kind of mutual love the Holy Spirit implants in us.

In conclusion, a personal confession. Five years ago a friend was intrigued by my admission that I had never known my grandparents' names. Her reaction? She began a Burghardt genealogy. Remarkable results, and still in process. At this moment some of the happy evidence is sitting here before my very eyes. . . . Alleluia![22]

17

Honoring
Conscientious Objectors

Expanding Our Vision of Veterans Day

In days to come
  the mountain of the Lord's house
shall be established as the highest of the mountains,
  and shall be raised above the hills. . . .
For out of Zion shall go forth instruction,
  and the word of the Lord from Jerusalem.
He shall judge between the nations,
  and shall arbitrate for many peoples;
they shall beat their swords into plowshares,
  and their spears into pruning hooks;
nation shall not lift up sword against nation,
neither shall they learn war any more.
—Isa. 2:2–4

Then he began to speak, and taught them, saying:
  "Blessed are the poor in spirit, for theirs is the kingdom of heaven.
  "Blessed are those who mourn, for they will be comforted.
  "Blessed are the meek, for they will inherit the earth.

93

"Blessed are those who hunger and thirst for righteousness, for they will be filled.

"Blessed are the merciful, for they will receive mercy.

"Blessed are the pure in heart, for they will see God.

"Blessed are the peacemakers, for they will be called children of God.

"Blessed are those who are persecuted for righteousness' sake, for theirs is the kingdom of heaven.

"Blessed are you when people revile you and persecute you and utter all kinds of evil against you falsely on my account."

—Matt. 5:2–11

I

It will help us if we begin with some background, historical and religious.

Often when looking at a painting of Ethan Allen's boys with their long-barreled muskets or hearing the hymn, "Onward Christian Soldiers Marching as to War,"[23] most of our images of those who serve in the military are filled with fighting and killing.

And yet in this country there is a long tradition of conscientious objection, the heartfelt, faith-filled tenet that killing another human being is wrong. From colonial times Brethren, Mennonites, Quakers, and Seventh-Day Adventists refused to be trained to fight and kill. Later they were joined by thousands of Catholics and other Christians of various denominations, as well as Muslims and Jewish men and women, who have individually petitioned as conscientious objectors not to fight. Some with others of like mind and heart have formed peace fellowships to support not only the nonmilitant soldiers but also these soldiers' families.

During the Civil War a revision to draft regulations had long-term implications for conscientious objectors. The new law indicated that objectors drafted into military service "be considered noncombatants." Abraham Lincoln made it policy to assign such noncombatants to duty in hospitals or in educating freed slaves and, thus, introduced alternate civilian service as an option for fulfilling one's military obligation. Unfortunately since that time, the country has not been consistent in paying for such service, and so too often objectors' families have suffered not only the hassle of neighbors who will not embrace conscientious objection as a matter of faith but also these families have suffered hunger when objectors have not been paid for their alternative civil work.[24]

II

Two realities merit special mention. First, what I have said does not mean that all conscientious objectors have avoided the battlefield. Many who have refused to fight have gone without guns into battle zones to rescue and nurse those who have been injured. In World War II a Seventh-Day Adventist conscientious objector was awarded a Medal of Honor for his heroism in Okinawa and a Southern Baptist conscientious objector posthumously was awarded a Medal of Honor for rescuing many soldiers in Vietnam.[25]

Second, the homeless veteran. True, President George W. Bush claims that under his administration federal spending for veterans has increased by more than two-thirds; medical treatments have been extended to a million additional veterans; and grants to homeless veterans across the country have been expanded. But in early November 2007, a study from the public nonprofit organization National Alliance to End Homelessness found that many former U.S. military personnel were slipping through the cracks — and they accounted for 25 percent of the nation's homeless population.[26]

For me, concern and confidence mingled when I learned from the Voice of America that in the fiscal year 2007 there were 24 million U.S. veterans living in our country and that our government spent $84 billion on programs for them, including almost $35 billion for health care.[27]

III

Finally, two quotations from leaders in church and state — strong remarks perhaps unexpected because of the centuries separating them but quite appropriate within the context of conscientious objection.

I have in mind Bishop Cyprian of Carthage writing to Donatus in the middle of the third century:

> Look down at the roads full of robbers, the sea infested with pirates and military bases spreading war and slaughter everywhere. It is a world wet with the blood of people slaughtering each other, where murder is regarded as a crime if committed by individuals but is called a public service when carried out *en masse,* as if it were not the question of innocence but the extent of the savagery that determines freedom from guilt.[28]

I have in mind as well a memorable observation by General Omar Bradley after World War II, when he was Administrator of Veterans Affairs: "We have grasped the mystery of the atom and rejected the Sermon on the Mount."[29]

Challenging material for preacher and congregation as they discover that the twenty-four hours on Veterans Day can hardly begin to do justice to the millions of veterans, men and women — yes, even conscientious objectors — who have served to preserve our homes and our way of life.

18

Thanks Be to God!

Thanksgiving Day or Every Day?

I will recount the gracious deeds of the Lord,
*   the praiseworthy acts of the Lord,*
because of all that the Lord has done for us,
*   and the great favor to the house of Israel*
that he has shown them according to his mercy,
*   according to the abundance of his steadfast love.*
For he said, "Surely they are my people,
*   children who will not deal falsely";*
and he became their savior in all their distress.
It was no messenger or angel
*   but his presence that saved them;*
in his love and in his pity he redeemed them;
*   he lifted them up and carried them all the days of old.*
*   — Isa. 63:7–9*

To the church of God that is in Corinth, to those who are sanc-
tified in Christ Jesus, called to be saints, together with all those
who in every place call on the name of our Lord Jesus Christ,
both their Lord and ours: Grace to you and peace from God
our Father and the Lord Jesus Christ. I give thanks to my God
always for you because of the grace of God that has been given

you in Christ Jesus, or in every way you have been enriched in him, in speech and knowledge of every kind — just as the testimony of Christ has been strengthened among you — so that you are not lacking in any spiritual gift as you wait for the revealing of our Lord Jesus Christ. — 1 Cor. 1:2–7

They came to the other side of the lake, to the country of the Gerasenes. And when he had stepped out of the boat, immediately a man out of the tombs with an unclean spirit met him. He lived among the tombs; and no one could restrain him any more, even with a chain. . . . [Jesus] had said to him, "Come out of the man, you unclean spirit!" Then Jesus asked him, "What is your name?" He replied, "My name is Legion; for we are many." He begged him earnestly not to send them out of the country. . . . As he was getting into the boat, the man who had been possessed by demons begged him that he might be with him. But Jesus refused, and said to him, "Go home to your friends, and tell them how much the Lord has done for you, and what mercy he has shown you." And he went away and began to proclaim in the Decapolis how much Jesus had done for him; and everyone was amazed. — Mark 5:1–3, 8–10, 18–20

Thanks, thanks, thanks. Arguably "thanks" is the monosyllable most frequently used in American speech. Of all words, I suspect that "thanks" is outrun only by "okay."

That piece of passing jollity simply carries us gently into exciting aspects of our call to be thanksgivers. For the three readings at the Thanksgiving Mass, the church allows choice from eleven texts of Sacred Scripture. The texts I have selected point to God's claims on our endless gratitude.

I

Begin with prophet Isaiah, who recalls "the gracious deeds of the Lord." What gracious deeds? "All that the Lord has done for us, and the great favor to the house of Israel that he has shown them according to his mercy" (Isa. 63:7).

The Lord said: "Surely they are my people, children who will not deal falsely"; and he became their savior in all their distress (v. 8). It was not a messenger or an angel, but he himself who saved them. Because of his love and pity he himself redeemed them, lifting them and carrying them all the days of old.

And what of us today, Americans in this century? We are living in a country that invaded another nation not in self-defense but as an act of aggression, an aggression that as I write has killed nearly four thousand Americans and more than a million Iraqis; an aggression that has wounded almost thirty thousand Americans and has left too many soldiers with mental problems; an aggression that already has lasted longer than World War II. This is how we best give thanks to a God of mercy who gives us opportunities again and again to use or misuse power?

II

Move now to St. Paul's prophesying in his letter to the Christians of Corinth. He is writing to men and women "sanctified in Christ Jesus, called to be [holy]" (1 Cor. 1:2). After conveying greetings of peace, Paul assures these persons that he gives thanks to God *always* on *their* account for the grace of God given to them in Christ

Jesus and reassures them that they are not lacking in any spiritual gift.

Additionally Paul reminds the Corinthians that "God is faithful, by Him [they] were called into the fellowship of his Son, Jesus Christ our Lord" (v. 9).

Spiritual gifts such as wisdom, faith, charity, intelligence, and hope are not given to benefit only an individual recipient. These gifts are for the betterment of all our brothers and sisters. Surely Paul's comment about fellowship with Jesus implies fellowship not only with God but also with other people. We can be confident that when Paul gives thanks for the gifts of others, he is cognizant that through fellowship, the gifts of one become the gifts of many.

A vivid example today of combining intelligence and charity is Muhammad Yunus, the recipient of the 2006 Nobel Peace Prize bestowed in recognition of his vision and implementation of microcredit — giving loans to some of the poorest persons on earth, those with no collateral whatsoever. Most of his seven million borrowers are women who have transformed not only their own families but entire villages. Change began through the compassion of one man who dared to loan money to people with no income. Surprising to many the repayment rate on these loans has been nearly 99 percent.

Yunus is keenly aware that poverty is a threat to peace. How will we use our spiritual gifts this day to lessen poverty in our own local community?

III

Now turn to one of Jesus' unexpected responses. Legion, an outcast who once had been bound with chains and shackles, had been living among the tombs. Finally having broken out of his chains he cried out to Jesus, "What have you to do with me?" (Mark 5:7ff.). Jesus' first unexpected response: "Come out of the man, you unclean spirit!" When others saw that Legion was suddenly again in his right mind, they were afraid and told more people what had happened.

Legion wanted to remain with Jesus and go by boat with him to Jesus' next destination. But Jesus would not let Legion go with him; instead he gave another surprising response, "Go home to your friends, and tell them how much the Lord has done for you." When Legion proclaimed what Jesus had done for him, all were amazed.

What did Jesus ask of Legion then and of us now? To be disciples — not literally to follow Jesus from town to town but rather to announce what God had done for Legion. Similarly for us, sharing the good news is not limited to reciting the Word of God but also sharing with others our thanks, our gratitude, for the many different gifts the Lord has given each of us.

19

A Priest in Every Season

A Sixty-Fifth-Year Homily

The spirit of the Lord God is upon me,
*   because the Lord has anointed me;*
he has sent me to bring good news to the oppressed,
*   to bind up the broken hearted,*
to proclaim liberty to the captives,
*   and release to the prisoners;*
to proclaim the year of the Lord's favor,
*   and the day of vengeance of our God....*
                                                                —Isa. 61:1–2

*   Pray then in this way:*
*   Our Father in heaven,*
*   hallowed be your name.*
*   Your kingdom come.*
*   Your will be done,*
*   on earth as it is in heaven.*
*   Give us this day our daily bread.*
*   And forgive us our debts,*
*   as we also have forgiven our debtors.*
*   And do not bring us to the time of trial,*
*   but rescue us from the evil one.*

For if you forgive others their trespasses, your heavenly Father will also forgive you; but if you do not forgive others, neither will your Father forgive your trespasses.   —Matt. 6:9–15

Today, as I close out six and a half decades of priestly existence, I shall not focus on myself alone or the past. Today I simply must dwell on *us* and the present. On every priest here at Manresa for reasons of health. Yes, me too.

The one all-important point of this homily? You and I are not "retired" priests. "Retired" comes down to us from the world of business — leaving a job and settling into a rocker. You and I have not retired — not from the priesthood, not even from priestly action.

Surprised? Don't be . . . for three splendid reasons. First, each day you and I can perform the most effective action within the church's power for channeling God's grace to the world, for the forgiveness of sins, for peace in the human heart. Yes, such is the incomparable power of the Eucharist, and it remains in your hands and mine, on your lips and mine. Retired? Not on your life — literally.

Move on now to a second reason. You see, our priestly activity does not end at noon. We are not isolated from "the world." We live twenty-four hours a day with a small but vibrant lay staff who form with us what some of us theologians would call a "little church." Together we are truly an enviable community, lay and cleric. A community of service, each to the other. From our sisters and brothers a wondrous service to our health, our well-being, our staying alive. And what service from you and me to them? Priestly service for which our very illnesses allow us time: to bless them and pray for them, to thank them and praise them, to counsel them and encourage them, to help them realize how Christlike their service is.

A third area for our priestly activity at Manresa is a gift from modern technology. Through e-mail you and I can touch the farthest reaches of God's earth — exchanging experiences and ideas, discussing religious problems, or just keeping in touch with other Jesuits like our cherished friend José Arroyo, who though far away in distant Spain is ever near in heart. Priestly too is a project of Vince O'Brien: a website, retreats, and conferences for separated and divorced Catholics. Equally priestly are the efforts of our "Poet in Residence," Tom Masterson, whose written fluid syllables raise our hearts in meter that few can equal with tongue or pen. I myself, despite my failing eyesight, am delighted that I can preach here and, with an uncommonly large magnifier and a special computer keyboard, compose articles for periodicals such as *America, The Living Pulpit*, and the *National Catholic Reporter.*

I suggest that another clear sign of continuing priestly activity would be more homilies from us priests here in Manresa. Each of us has years of experience, love of Scripture, a rich background of Ignatian spirituality. Let's share all this with one another. If necessary or if more comfortable, let your wheelchair be your pulpit!

More could be added about priesthood in action at Manresa. But perhaps enough has been said to convince you (if you need convincing) that we are not "retired" priests. In the very midst of our varied illnesses we are *doing* Eucharistic liturgy now as we did before we came to Manresa; we are engaged *every* day in a very human way with people, clergy and laity.

Like you, my friends, I did not choose this way of living out my priesthood. Not for my sixty-fifth anniversary! Yet still I rejoice. For I am blest with the companionship of Jesuits who carry the cross of Christ with courage, dignity, and even a certain measure of joy. Blest too with the support of a staff for whom service is not an imposition but a God-given privilege.

For all this, and for much else still unspoken, my ongoing gratitude to our dear Lord by whose grace we do not retire from our priestly activity "for the greater glory of God."

20

Courage in the Dark

A Jesuit's Diamond Jubilee

With what shall I come before the Lord,
and bow myself before God most high? . . .
He has told you, O mortal, what is good;
and what does the Lord require of you
but to do justice, and to love kindness,
and to walk humbly with your God?
— Mic. 6:6, 8

Immediately he made the disciples get into the boat and go
on ahead to the other side, while he dismissed the crowds. And
after he had dismissed the crowds, he went up the mountain by
himself to pray. . . . And early in the morning he came walking
toward them on the sea. But when the disciples saw him walking
on the sea, they were terrified, saying, "It is a ghost!" And they
cried out in fear. But immediately Jesus spoke to them and said,
"Take heart, it is I; do not be afraid."
— Matt. 14:22–23, 25–27

Some years ago a bishop in Connecticut opened his homily
with these words: "As King Henry VIII said to each of his

This homily was expanded and published as the cover story, "Courage: Absence
of Fear or Grace under Pressure?" in the *National Catholic Reporter,* July 14, 2006.

wives, 'I shall not keep you very long.'" Nor shall I. Still, on this seventy-fifth anniversary of my unheralded descent on the Society of Jesus, I dare to share with you three ideas, three words, that are particularly precious to me at this hour. They concern the past, the present, and the future — yesterday, today, and tomorrow.

The first word — from the past, from yesterday — is THANKS. Its high importance cries aloud to me at the beginning of the Preface in the Latin Mass: *Vere dignum et iustum est.* . . . "It is truly fitting and a matter of justice that we give praise and thanks to God always and everywhere." A far cry from our English-language version "We do well." We indeed do well, but precisely because not to thank God always and everywhere is a sin against justice.

And so I thank God for giving me life. I thank Christ our Lord for wearing my flesh, living and dying for me, blessing me with his very self in Holy Communion. I thank the divine Spirit dwelling within me as the Light shattering my human darkness.

I thank God for my mother and father. Immigrants from Austria-Hungary, they lived and labored for my brother and me. They never spoke in German to us. One exception — when Pop said to me, *Du bist ein Esel* ("You're a jackass").

I thank God for the Society of Jesus, which has opened a wondrous way of life for me, an incomparable spirituality in the *Spiritual Exercises* of St. Ignatius, a companionship of like-minded men hard to equal for inspiration.

I thank God for an uncountable number of the laity, men and women (some here today), whose admirable lives, whose friendship and love, have helped immensely to make me a more caring priest, a more dynamic Jesuit, a more human person—even a more open theologian.

My second word (actually three words) touches today, the present. It is a strong exhortation: LIVE THIS DAY!

Take my own experience. Several years ago I learned that I am afflicted with wet macular degeneration. An expert in the field told me that mine was among the worst cases he had ever seen. Within eighteen months I had no vision at all in my right eye, and the disease was progressing in my left eye. At this moment I see only through an increasingly hazy left eye. At ninety-one my mind is still clear, even as memory all too often plays me false on facts and faces. But a clear mind without eyes? And hearing loss to boot?

How have I come to grips with this experience? Three momentous monosyllables: Live this day! Yesterday is a memory, tomorrow a dream. Today is the only day I actually live. And so I begin each day with the selfsame prayer: "Dear Lord, grace me to live this day as if it is my first day, my last day, my only day." All the while I offer my frustrations and failures to God for the helpless, the homeless, and the hopeless in our unjust world.

My third word — a word for the future, for tomorrow — is COURAGE. I cannot forget a remark made to me half a century ago by John Courtney Murray: "Courage, Walter! It's far more important than intelligence." This from one of the most intelligent humans of the twentieth century. Why so important for us at Manresa? Because for many of us there is no cure for our primary problem—we are aging—and time is our enemy. Health problems can *dis*-courage. In contrast, listen to a woman whose cancer threatened to overwhelm her: "The more courage I used to get through the day, the more courage I had. The more I embraced life — relationships, nature, and the joys of every day — the richer my life became."

What precisely is this courage? It is *not* the absence of fear. It is feeling afraid to do something but finding the strength to do it. Where find the strength? Some find it in resources deep within themselves; others get it from a God-given grace, an answer to prayer.

I suspect that my courage stems from both sources. A prime example is this homily. For over six decades, without exception I preached from a carefully prepared text; not that I read it but it was there if I needed it. Today I again have a carefully prepared text but this time without the eyes and memory of old. What if I stumble over words, forget what comes next, make a fool of myself? But here I am, and whatever the result, I had the strength to try. I hope and pray that some of my Manresa brothers will be tempted to preach at our daily liturgy and will have the strength to yield to that temptation.

A final word, a word for tomorrow, to the dear friends who have come from near and far to rejoice with me. There must be times, will be times, when you are afraid to do something important — afraid to love, afraid to give or forgive, afraid to cry out against injustice. For courage, reach. Reach into your deepest self and reach for the Christ who, St. Ignatius insisted, works "like a laborer" with you, within you.

Good friends all: (1) I THANK you with all my heart for your friendship, your love, and your inspiration. (2) I hope that with God's grace you will always LIVE THIS DAY. (3) I pray that in fearful situations true COURAGE will mark your reactions. In return, I ask only an occasional prayer that, despite the degeneration of eyes, I may continue to write, preach, and clamor against global injustice. For, as a friend insists, though I am losing my sight, *I have not lost my vision!*

21

Jubilee for Two Priests

Sixtieth and Sixty-Fifth
Ordination Celebration

*Now if Christ is proclaimed as raised from the dead, how can
some of you say there is no resurrection of the dead? If there is
no resurrection of the dead, then Christ has not been raised;
and if Christ has not been raised, then our proclamation has
been in vain and your faith has been in vain.*

— 1 Cor. 15:12–14

*Now after John was arrested, Jesus came to Galilee, proclaiming
the good news of God, and saying, "The time is fulfilled, and
the kingdom of God has come near; repent, and believe in the
good news." As Jesus passed along the Sea of Galilee, he saw
Simon and his brother Andrew casting a net into the sea —
for they were fishermen. And Jesus said to them, "Follow me
and I will make you fish for people." And immediately they left
their nets and followed him. As he went a little farther, he saw
James son of Zebedee and his brother John, who were in their
boat mending the nets. Immediately he called them; and they*

This liturgy celebrated the sixtieth anniversary of the ordination of Edward H.
Nash, S.J., and the sixty-fifth anniversary of the ordination of Walter J.
Burghardt, S.J.

left their father Zebedee in the boat with the hired men, and
followed him. — Mark 1:14–20

Our Manresa liturgy today celebrates priesthood. Not the priesthood of all the faithful; simply the priesthood of the ordained. And our focus is on two priests of this community — Father Edward Nash, ordained sixty years ago, and your homilist, ordained sixty-five years ago. Hence my three points: a word on Father Nash, a word on myself, a word on Manresa.

I

First, Father Nash. Two years after his ordination, Ed — along with six other Jesuits — set sail from New York City to Bombay, India. The crossing took one month with no stops along the way. After six months in Gomoh to learn Hindi, Ed made many stops in villages between Chaibasa and Dhanbad. Usually he traveled on a motorcycle, which also served as his altar when Ed offered Mass at the homes of lepers living in makeshift huts furnished only with sleeping mats. There were times when Ed offered as many as twenty-two Masses in a week, often traveling two hundred miles on Sunday to serve villages situated many miles from each other.

His trips were complicated not only by weather but also by goats, bears, and other animals in the road. Yet Ed is fond of saying that in his more than half a century in India, "There was never an assignment I found difficult." In baseball parlance, he calls himself "a utility infielder" — filling in wherever his broad talents for ministry were needed.

II

Second, myself. On the whole, a significantly different approach to ministry. Although I never encountered a single goat or bear, I, too, traveled extensively, especially in my program Preaching the Just Word, a retreat/workshop given more than a hundred times across the United States and in Canada and Australia. Still, my major preoccupation has been and remains theology, a continuing quest for deeper understanding of God, of God's people, of God's earth. This preoccupation revealed itself in a number of ways: as editor of the journal *Theological Studies,* as author of 24 books and more than 350 articles, as a member of the papal International Theological Commission, and in teaching patristic theology at Woodstock College and at the Catholic University of America.

I see no conflict between Ed's "circuit rider priesthood" and my endeavors in teaching and preaching, in research and publication. Both of us were striving to meet actual needs in the worldwide church. Very simply, some needs of the church can be met from a motorcycle, others at a computer.

III

My third point, Manresa Hall. After six decades and more, Ed and I find ourselves here at Manresa. Not a silent hermitage, not a home only for the aged, not primarily a place to die.

Both when we entered the Society and again when we came to Manresa, we came to a Jesuit community. And a *genuine* Jesuit community is not only a place where a group of Jesuits eat together. It is a home where we get to know each other, where we care for one another, where we talk and listen to one another, where we encourage one another, where we laugh and grieve together, where we exchange stories and memories, ideas and jokes.

In closing, I suggest a prayer and a proposal. A prayer of thanksgiving to God for a competent and compassionate staff, a staff that provides much of the strength we need to lead productive lives. A proposal that we Jesuits will continue with heart and soul to strengthen the community here at Manresa, rejoicing in the words St. Peter said to Jesus on the Mount of Transfiguration, "Lord, it is good for us to be here" (see Matt. 17:4 and Mark 9:5).

PART FIVE

TRIBUTE

22

Scholar, Author, Preacher

Funeral Homily for Walter J. Burghardt, S.J.

We are gathered at this Eucharist to express our thanks to God for the birth of our great and good friend Walter Burghardt into eternal life. And we do so by recalling with gratitude the many gifts that Walter shared with us, gifts that God first shared with him. In emulation of Walter, I list those graces in three points:

First, Walter was an extraordinarily gifted scholar and author, teacher and preacher.

Second, he was a man of childlike simplicity — truly a son of God.

Third, he was passionately committed to the promotion of social justice in our world.

First, Walter was an extraordinarily gifted scholar and author, teacher and preacher.

Walter Burghardt's career reads like a listing in a *Who's Who.* For thirty-two years Walter taught patristics and historical theology at Woodstock College outside Baltimore, then in New York, and subsequently at Catholic University and Georgetown University. He was a visiting lecturer at Union

Theological Seminary, New York (1971–74) and Princeton Theological Seminary (1972–73). He was appointed twice to the International Theological Commission by Pope Paul VI. Ecumenism was one of Walter's loves and talents. He was a member of the U.S. Dialogue Group called Lutheran-Roman Catholic Conversations (1965–76) and was a member of the Faith and Order Commission of the World Council of Churches (1968–76).

For twenty-three years he was editor-in-chief of *Theological Studies*, the foremost Catholic theological journal in the United States. He was coeditor of the series of translations entitled *Ancient Christian Writers,* and was also cofounder and coeditor of *The Living Pulpit*, an ecumenical journal on preaching.

In the course of his career, he published 24 books (this book is his 25th) and more than 350 articles in over 70 journals. His memoir *Long Have I Loved You: A Theologian Reflects on His Church*, was awarded a first prize by the Catholic Press Association. He received honorary degrees from twenty-three colleges or universities. In 1996 a two-year Baylor University survey named him one of the twelve "most effective preachers" in the English-speaking world; he was the only Catholic among the twelve.

And he did everything with style, with panache, with sophistication. Anyone who heard him preach — and I'm sure most of us have — knew they were in the presence of a master. We were taken by his poise and bearing, his theological insight and turn of phrase, his wit and humor, his store of knowledge and command of history.

One reaction to Walter's death is typical of thousands. It came from my brother Marty, who, as a former Jesuit scholastic, had Walter in class. He e-mailed me, "I'm sorry to hear that Walter Burghardt died yesterday. Not for him, of course, but for the void he'll leave. As I've often told you, the courses I took from him as a young twerp at Woodstock (Plato's *Republic* and St. Augustine's *Confessions*) were a truly formative experience."

But for all his brilliance and sophistication, Walter was childlike at heart. And that is my second point.

Second, Walter was a man of childlike simplicity — truly a son of God.

For all his brilliance, bearing, and elegance, he had a wonderful simplicity about him. And this is what made him so appealing and such a good friend. It was a fascinating combination: his sophisticated bearing and his childlike simplicity.

Those who saw him only in the pulpit would have had no idea of how nervous he was in the sacristy just before Mass. He was like a student sweating it out before an oral exam. His suavity in the pulpit was matched only by his insecurity in the sacristy.

He was also a hypochondriac. To hear him talk, you'd think he had suffered from every disease known to man or woman, and yet here he was pushing sixty, then seventy, then eighty, and finally the nineties. In one of his short autobiographical pieces near the end of his life he wrote:

> I shall not dwell on the loss of my father and only brother [only sibling] within three weeks of each other. I have to confess, however, that their deaths, both of cancer, have played a significant role in my

development as a state-of-the-art hypochondriac. No one in human history, to my knowledge, has experienced as many fatal symptoms as I (*On Turning Eighty: Autobiography in Search of Meaning*).

As he aged, Walter also became much more open and free in the acknowledgement of his sinfulness and human weakness, and his need for God's forgiving love. And God's forgiveness was the source of his profound gratitude to God, which he expressed over and over — in conversation, in his memoirs and letters, and in his prayer.

Finally, I think that, to a large degree, it was his childlike simplicity, openness, and clarity of gaze that enabled Walter to discern and discover the final, major phase of his life: the program called "Preaching the Just Word." And that's the third and final point of this homily.

Third, Walter was passionately committed to the promotion of social justice in our world.

When Walter was approaching eighty years of age he decided to step down as editor-in-chief of *Theological Studies*. He came to see me one day and his question was, "What should I do now?" We talked a long time and certain things seem to come clear: it ought to have something to do with preaching. Second, it ought to have something to do with the contemporary mission of the Society of Jesus, namely, serving faith by promoting justice. Finally, its influence should be as widespread as possible. "Think about this," Walter said. "Every Sunday in the United States thousands of preachers are speaking to millions of people in the pews.

Imagine the impact for the good of society if these homilies inspired all those people to engage serious issues of social justice and to work to heal them."

That conversation gave birth to the five-day retreat/ workshop called "Preaching the Just Word" (PJW), which Walter and his friend diocesan priest Raymond Kemp led and in which a number of you here have been presenters and participants. Many more than a hundred retreat/ workshops have been offered in practically every diocese in the United States and also in Australia, Jamaica, and Canada. Just imagine the miles that Walter logged — and all of this while in his eighties and young nineties — and also while he was gradually losing his sight because of wet macular degeneration.

In 2004 Walter published a book inspired by his multi-year experience with "Preaching the Just Word." It is entitled *Justice: A Global Adventure*. Especially moving, he often said, were the stories of heroic service to the poor told by priests and religious making the retreat/workshop. The book is dedicated to Raymond Baker Kemp and also to Marian Wright Edelman and her colleagues at the Children's Defense Fund.

In all of this we see how Christlike Walter became. He exemplified in his own life the principal qualities we find in Jesus' own life. Look at the Scriptures:

First, *an extraordinarily gifted teacher and preacher.* At Jesus' first homily at Nazareth the people marveled. "Where does he get all this?" they asked. And others would say, "He speaks as one having authority!" So too of Walter.

Second, *childlike.* Jesus said over and over, "Unless you become as a little child you cannot not enter the Kingdom of heaven." And that's how Jesus behaved in reliance upon his Abba, Father. So too did Walter.

Third, *passionate for justice*. Jesus said, "Unless your justice surpasses that of the scribes and Pharisees you will not enter the kingdom of heaven — so be just as your heavenly Father is just." And so Walter was.

As we pray for Walter, let's ask Walter to be praying for us,

* that in word and deed we might teach others God's goodness as Walter did,

* that we might live with the simplicity of God's children as Walter did, and

* that we might work with Walter's generosity and courage to make our world more just, loving, and peaceful.

And this prayer we make in the name of Jesus the Lord. AMEN.

James L. Connor, S.J.
Holy Trinity Catholic Church
Washington, D.C.
February 20, 2008

Notes

1. Ben-Zion Gold, *The Life of Jews in Poland before the Holocaust* (Lincoln: University of Nebraska Press, 2007) 24–25.

2. For a 2009 chart of "Frequently Requested Catholic Church Statistics," see *http://cara.georgetown.edu/bulletin/index.htm*.

3. Sparta, New Jersey, is the town of the groom's youth.

4. See Evelyn Whitehead and James Whitehead, "Christian Marriage," *U.S. Catholic* 47, no. 6 (June 1982) 9.

5. Hyacinth M. Cordell, O.P., "Why '*Gaudete?*'" *www.freerepublic.com/focus/f-religion/1939268/posts*.

6. This story has been recounted many times over the years; "my" version is based on a rendition by Marian Wright Edelman, founder and president of the Children's Defense Fund.

7. For a succinct history of this Christian season, see M. F. Connell, "Epiphany, The Solemnity of," *New Catholic Encyclopedia*, 2nd ed., 5 (2003) 293–95.

8. Daniel J. Harrington, S.J., "Particular and Universal: The Epiphany of the Lord (C)," *America* 196, no. 1 (January 1–8, 2007) 30.

9. Joseph A. Fitzmyer, S.J., *The Gospel according to Luke I–IX* (Garden City, N.Y.: Doubleday, 1981) 335.

10. Ibid. 337–38.

11. *The New American Bible,* Saint Joseph edition (New York: Catholic Book Publishing Co., 1992) 212. The same work goes on to assert: "The entire history of the conquest of the Promised Land is a prophecy of the spiritual conquest of the world through the Church under the leadership of Jesus the Messiah."

12. For a thorough discussion of this problem, see Joseph A. Fitzmyer, S.J., *The Gospel according to Luke X–XXIV* (New York: Doubleday, 1985) 1443–44.

13. See *2007 Catalog of the Provinces of the Society of Jesus in the United States of America* (privately published, St. Louis, Mo.) 133–34.

14. Bob Herbert, "The Danger Zone," *New York Times,* March 15, 2007, A27. This Op-Ed column merits being read in its entirety.

15. Joseph J. Fahey, "A Hopeful People: Changes for the Better Are Taking Place in Venezuela," *America* 195, no. 15 (November 13, 2006) 17–20, at 17.

16. Joseph A. Fitzmyer, S.J., *The Acts of the Apostles,* Anchor Bible 31 (New York: Doubleday, 1998) 232.

17. Ibid. 248.

18. Daniel J. Harrington, S.J., "Openness to the Holy Spirit," *America* 196, no. 16 (May 7, 2007) 47.

19. Carl R. Kazmierski, "John the Baptist," *The Modern Catholic Encyclopedia* (Collegeville, Minn.: Liturgical Press, 2004) 444.

20. Walter J. Burghardt, S.J., *Saints and Sanctity* (Englewood Cliffs, N.J.: Prentice-Hall, 1965).

21. This aphorism attributed to G. K. Chesterton is frequently cited as, "A saint is one who exaggerates what the world neglects." For the rendition cited in this homily, see Max L. Christensen, *Heroes and Saints: More Stories of People Who Made a Difference* (Louisville: Westminster John Knox, 1997) 17.

22. This homily was delivered to direct descendants and collateral relatives of Johann Jacob Burghardt, the first Burghardt in my direct line to emigrate from Ketsch, Germany, to Padew Narodowa, Austria-Hungary. Present were family members from Maryland, Massachusetts, New Jersey, New York, Pennsylvania, South Carolina, Wisconsin, and Germany.

23. This hymn was not a military song in origin but rather a song for use in an annual Anglican procession of children marching from one parish to another. For a fuller discussion, see "Great Hymns of the Faith," *www.faithepc.org/Sermons/1999/990919.htm.*

24. For a fuller discussion of the history of conscientious objection in the United States, see Peter Shapiro, *A History of National Service in America* (College Park, Md.: Center for Political Leadership and Participation, 1994).

25. Edward F. Murphy, "A Conscientious Objector's Medal of Honor," *Vietnam* magazine, June 2003.

26. "In 2005, veterans made up 11 percent of the adult population, but 26 percent of the homeless population. This was reported by Mary Cunningham, Meghan Henry, and Webb Lyons in their November 2007

report, "Vital Mission: Ending Homelessness among Veterans." For the entire report, see *www.endhomelessness.org/content/article/detail/1837.*

27. For statistics on veterans and homeless, see notes from the 2006 conference "Ending Homelessness among Veterans through Permanent Supportive Housing," *www.voa.org/portals/40/veterans-leadership-dialogue -final-web.pdf.*

28. Cyprian of Carthage, *Letter to Donatus, 1.6.*

29. From Bradley's Armistice Day speech in Boston (November 11, 1948), *Collected Writings,* vol. 1, 1967.